THE HERETIC

THE HERETIC

A Play in Three Acts by

MORRIS L. WEST

William Morrow and Company, Inc., New York

Illustrations by Terry M. Fehr

Preface

It is the illusion of our time that the non-conformist is in the ascendant, that the heretic is the hero and the revolutionary is the new redeemer.

In fact, the odd man out has never been so much at risk or so competently menaced by that conspiracy of power which we are pleased to call government.

The mechanics of social control are more sophisticated than they have ever been in history, most sophisticated in those countries where the legal and judicial odds seem loaded in favour of the individual.

The Marxist position is at least clear: deviate and you are damned—to expulsion from the Party, to breadline subsistence, to a limbo of non-persons, to a brutal confinement, to death without honour. The democratic method is more subtle but hardly less effective. The taxing authority may invade your most private transactions, and what it cannot prove it may presume, in default of contrary evidence. An employer may solicit, file and transmit, without your consent, the most intimate details of your private life—and your refusal to communicate them may provide a presumption of hidden delinquencies. The social spy, the wiretapper, the pedlar of devices to violate privacy have become stock personages in our society. The growth of large monopolies in communication has forced the protestor into the streets and the parks, where his protest may easily be construed or manipulated into a public disorder. A whole industry has been built round the art of affirmation, but the dignity of dissent is daily denigrated, the doubter is in disgrace because he demands time to reflect before he commits himself to an act of faith, and the liberty most laborious to maintain is the liberty to be mistaken.

But the threat to the odd man out is not merely an external one. It is internal as well. So much diverse information, so many divergent opinions are poured into his eyes and ears that the effort to rationalise them all threatens, at times, his very sanity. Often his only salvation is to call a halt, to say: "I do not know. I cannot commit until I do know. I will not commit without the time and the freedom which you refuse to grant me."

I myself have been caught in this syncope. I myself have been subject to the most artful and powerful pressures to force me to proclaim that which others believe to be true, but which I cannot in good conscience profess.

This is why I wrote the story of Giordano Bruno, dead and burned for heresy three hundred and seventy years ago. I could not believe that any man should be required to sell his soul—however undeveloped—to anyone who promised him order, discipline, social acceptance and three meals a day.

I had walked a hundred times past the brooding statue of Bruno in the Campo dei Fiori in Rome. I had searched out his works and collated the fragmentary records of his trials in Venice and in Rome. I had found him, like all of us, a contradictory character: a muddled philosopher, an arrogant scholar, a boaster and a poet, scared, venal, compromising, and yet, in sum, a figure of heroic proportions. He recanted once, after a short inquisition in Venice, and then, after seven years in the hands of the Roman inquisition, refused a second recantation which would have saved his life and would perhaps have given him back his liberty.

I found myself in him: my fears, my doubts, my own wrongheadedness, my conviction that, soon or late, a man has to know a reason for living or dying. The reason may be wrong, but man's right to hold the reason is inalienable. I wrote a play because in a book it is all too easy to succumb to the treacherous balance of rationality. I wrote in verse because I could express in no other way the turmoil of my own spirit. I wrote what I felt and what I believed, and I cared not then, and I care not now, how the writing is received.

I am on record now, through the friendship and co-operation of my publishers. I hope, one day, a great actor may see Bruno as I see him, and play him as I wrote him. If not, so be it! I have walked for a space in a dark land and, thanks to Bruno, I have survived the experience and live now a little humbler and much richer in endurance.

MORRIS L. WEST
Sardinia, July, 1969.

Cast

GIORDANO BRUNO, *a wandering Scholar*

PRIOR GABRIELLI, *Inquisitor General of Venice*

GIOVANNI MOCENIGO, *a Venetian Nobleman*

DONA DARIA, *Mocenigo's wife*

LUDOVICO TAVERNA, *Papal Nuncio to the Venetian Republic*

TOMMASSO MOROSINI, *Assessor of the Venetian Republic*

BORTOLO, *Mocenigo's Servant*

LAURENTIO PRIOLI, *the Patriarch of Venice*

A RECORDER *of the Venetian Inquisition*

A BARBER *of the Roman Inquisition*

A GAOLER *of the Roman Inquisition*

A NOTARY *of the Roman Inquisition*

Curial Officials, Guards, Gaolers, and others.

THE TIME: *1592–1600*

THE PLACE: *Venice and Rome*

"*Fides suadenda non imponenda.*
[Faith must be persuaded, never imposed.]"

BERNARD OF CLAIRVAUX

"Much have I struggled. I thought
    I would be able to conquer . . .
And both fate and nature repressed my
    zeal and my strength.
Even to have come forth is something,
    since I see that being able to conquer
Is placed in the hands of fate. However,
    there was in me
Whatever I was able to do, that which
    no future century
Will deny to be mine, that which a victor
    could have for his own:
Not to have feared to die, not to have
    yielded to any equal
In firmness of nature, and to have preferred
    a courageous death to
A noncombatant life."

GIORDANO BRUNO—*De Monade*

ACT ONE

Scene I

[*Venice, 1591. The library of the palace of* GIOVANNI
MOCENIGO, *scion of a family which to this date has produced a
number of doges, a great admiral and many statesmen. A gallery
runs across the rear of the room, and a staircase leads down to the
stage level. There is one entrance from the gallery and another at
the rear of the room. There is a large fireplace, over which hangs
the portrait of the last Mocenigo Doge, Alvise II. There is a window alcove from which one looks down upon the traffic of the
Grand Canal. The casement is open to the sunset glow. The
sound of the city drifts in: the cries of the pedlars, the chant of the
gondoliers, laughter, the shouts of revellers, a motley of music, the
growl of approaching thunder.*

GIOVANNI MOCENIGO *stands in the alcove, looking down at
the spectacle. He is a man in his mid-thirties, tall, lean, tor-
mented. He turns abruptly with a gesture of disgust.*]

MOCENIGO
          Venice! A stinking city!
Dabbling like a duck in its own ordure,
Pecking at fruit-rinds, cabbage-stalks and turds,
Ripe-rotten peaches, fish-heads, turnip-tops,

3

Dead cats and sodden bread and bloated meat,
Slops from the whore-house windows—Venice!

[*He crosses to the table on which is set an ornate carafe of wine and jewelled goblets. He pours wine and makes an ironic toast to the portrait of the Doge Alvise.*]

To your city, Uncle!

[*He drinks, draining the cup. The storm bursts in a clap of thunder and a gust of wind that slams the casements. He hurries to lock them and draw the drapes.*]

        Bortolo! Lights! God's blood!
Where are you, man?

[BORTOLO, *an elderly servant, hurries in with a taper and lights the candles.* MOCENIGO *pours more wine and drinks compulsively. The storm rises outside.*]

BORTOLO
        That should slack their lute strings!
Wash off some patches, send some gallants home
With sopping breeches!

MOCENIGO
        Gallants! My God! The Turks
Are creeping back. Spain and the Austrians snap
About our flanks. And they make love-play,
Suck on my lady's tits and fumble at her skirts
After the boatmen have invaded her!
Where is our revered counsellor, the Prior?

BORTOLO
[*a double-edged gesture*]
With Dona Daria!

MOCENIGO
There's a clever one!
Secret as the grave, suave as silk.
A prayer book for my wife. For me a prod,
A tiny dagger prick to say—"Where Peter is,
There is the Church. And where the Church,
There are the Dogs of God, to sniff out heresy,
Confound the over-wise, bring down the high
—Who, out of favour with the Ten, have yet
No friends in Rome . . ."
[*a note of menace*]
I trust you, my Bortolo.

BORTOLO
I am deaf, my lord.

MOCENIGO
And will be dumb, if you
Breathe but a word of what you do not hear.

BORTOLO
Supper, my lord?

MOCENIGO
I wait a guest.

BORTOLO
The storm
Will hold him.

5

MOCENIGO

[*laughs*]

No! He needs the meal, the bed,
A friend. These scholars are a hungry lot.
This one a little hungrier than most,
Therefore the more serviceable. Dona Daria
Must be prayed out. Entreat the worthy Prior
To give her a special blessing and join me here.

BORTOLO

My lord! . . .

[*He exits.* MOCENIGO *crosses to the picture of his uncle and stands facing it.*]

MOCENIGO

Where are you now, Uncle? In heaven?
Or a private gilded hell for doges
And the Decimal Councillors of this
Our Most Serene Republic? Where? I would like
To know. Up there? It would be blasphemy
To spit in your angelic eye and say,
"You lost us Nicosia, Famagusta,
And to me you lost all hope of eminence,
All favour of my peers." Down there? Better!
I could with a little magic—which I hope
To learn!—summon you up on summer evenings,
Let you stroll, invisible of course,
Among the whores in the Piazza, breathe
For a little while the cool from the lagoon,
Savour the sunset splendour, hear the chink
Of honest gold among the changers' booths,
The sighs of lovers in the gondolas—

6

And then? A foot in your face to thrust you back
Into the sulphur; an ear cupped to hear
You sizzle in the frypan, crying: "Giovanni!
Nephew Giovanni! Save me!" I would not
To save myself, save you, old man, one twitch
Of an eternity of dolours! Do you know
What you have done?

[*At this moment,* PRIOR GABRIELLI, *the Dominican, enters and
stands listening.*]

               You have castrated me!
Made me a chirping cantor in the choir
When once I might have shouted down Saint Mark's,
And set the lions trembling on their pedestals.

PRIOR GABRIELLI
You could again, my lord . . . !

[MOCENIGO *whirls to face him.*]

MOCENIGO
You intrude, Prior!

PRIOR GABRIELLI
[*calm*]
No! I was called. I came. The bruised spirit
Cries out in torment. I am fortunate
To hear the cry—a confessional confidence,
Believe me!—I am a doctor of sick souls,
I dispense the soothing balm of faith
And hope and Christian charity.

7

[MOCENIGO, *recovering himself, crosses to the wine flagon.*]

MOCENIGO
Wine?

PRIOR GABRIELLI
A small cup—for the stomach's sake!

[MOCENIGO *pours wine and hands him the cup.*]

To peace
In the house of Mocenigo!

MOCENIGO
I count on you
To bring it, Prior.

[*They drink.*]

My wife is chastely shriven?

PRIOR GABRIELLI
Your wife is a noble spirit, purified
By daily sacraments, by prayer, good works
—And by a singular forbearance! Virtue
Goes out from her.

MOCENIGO
God's blood! And how it goes!
And goes and goes!

PRIOR GABRIELLI
Do you wish to confess?

MOCENIGO

Not yet! I need a preparation. Time
To fill up a tally of more manly sins
Before I kneel in penitence.

PRIOR GABRIELLI
My lord,
There is no guarantee of time. Our God
Is not a banker signing notes of credit
Upon our promises.

MOCENIGO
[*cheerful again*]
Well said, good Prior!
On the other hand, God does make bargains
With his chosen ones. God's vicar, he
Who sits in Rome on Peter's throne and wears
The ring of Peter—he makes bargains, too.
He binds, he loosens, he lifts up, puts down.
He is the servant, is he not, of those
Who serve God's cause.

PRIOR GABRIELLI
It is his proudest title.

MOCENIGO

So! We can bargain. You for him. And I
For restoration of my house and name
To a high office in the Serenissima
—The Doge's cap, perhaps, or better yet,
A seat in the High Council of the Ten.
Think on that, Prior!

PRIOR GABRIELLI
I am thinking.
I ask how Rome can speak in the cabals
Of Venice.

MOCENIGO
She can. Red hats and bishoprics,
Abbacies, priories—these are tongues of fire!

PRIOR GABRIELLI
I ask then what could Mocenigo do
That others could not, would not, for the Pope.

MOCENIGO
What others? Number them on your sacred hands.
Spell out their names—Falieri, Contarini,
All the rest. Will they give Rome one ship,
One gun, one man, one ducat for defence
Against the Turks? Will they denounce a Switzer
Calvinist, a Lutheran from Mainz,
A vile Waldensian, an English lord
Reeking of heresy and tobacco smoke?
So long as they have trade to make—never!

PRIOR GABRIELLI
[dry]
But a Mocenigo would be different?

MOCENIGO
A grateful Mocenigo. Yes.

PRIOR GABRIELLI
My lord,

I am your friend and I believe you—but
In Rome they believe only in God.

MOCENIGO

                    And He,
To make them so believe, rose from the dead.

PRIOR GABRIELLI
[laughs]

Can you do that?

MOCENIGO
[savage]

                Rise from the dead? No!
But out of this limbo, yes!

PRIOR GABRIELLI
Without Rome?

MOCENIGO

With or without! You choose!

PRIOR GABRIELLI

                        Make me an offer,
Give me one gift in hand that says to Rome,
"Giovanni Mocenigo is a man
Of power and possibility for the Church.
Lift him and Rome is lifted—one fulcrum
For a double hoist . . ."

MOCENIGO
[satisfied at last]

                Good! Now, tell me, Prior,

What is Rome's greatest fear? What gives the Pope
More night-mares than bad sausage?

PRIOR GABRIELLI
                                        Heresy!
The rending of the seamless robe of truth.
This rabble of mountebanks and maguses
Who shout reform, defile the Eucharist,
Flout all authority, elect false bishops,
Deny the Trinity and saving grace,
Abolish marriage, set their private minds
Against the long tradition of the Faith
And Peter's dictates and the Holy Writ . . .

MOCENIGO
But they flourish, Prior. Why?

PRIOR GABRIELLI
                                    They are a plague,
A dancing madness!

MOCENIGO
People like to dance.

PRIOR GABRIELLI
And every prince would like to be Pope,
And every clown a Plato!

MOCENIGO
So, the cure?

PRIOR GABRIELLI
Obedience in humble faith.

MOCENIGO
Enforced

By whom?

PRIOR GABRIELLI
Induced by prayer.

MOCENIGO
They pray in Zurich,

But against the Pope.

PRIOR GABRIELLI
That is a blasphemy,

And blasphemy is criminal. A Christian prince
Must rule for God, from whom his power flows.
He must burn out impurities with fire,
Rack, rend and quite destroy God's enemies.

MOCENIGO

There is your gift in hand, Prior. Myself!
A hammer against heresy! But not,
As I am now, hung on the smithy wall
For want of arms to swing me! A bargain, yes?

PRIOR GABRIELLI

I cannot bargain for the Pope. I can
Provide a prelude . . .

MOCENIGO
[eagerly comic]
Well composed? Sweet strings

Of lutes? Viols and mandolas? Fiddlers,
Tambourines and flutes?

PRIOR GABRIELLI
If you can pay,
My lord—a choir of angels!

MOCENIGO
[*following the paranoid comedy*]
                  Name the price!
A fresco for your priory? Tintoretto's old
But good—God's blood, he's good! An altarcloth
Of pearls? A mass-cup, gold on crysoprase?
Titles of land in perpetuity?
Name it!

PRIOR GABRIELLI
[*carefully*]
A caution here! The gifts of piety
Are rich in merit. But from prince to Pope,
What is another jewel more or less,
Another pumpkin patch? The offering
Should speak a thousand words by silence, show
Heart's reasons at a glance, and make a pact
In secret that no notary could frame,
No prudent prince could ratify.
You take my meaning?

MOCENIGO
I do. And I am grateful.
I will think on it.

[BORTOLO *enters with an announcement.*]

BORTOLO
Your guest, my lord.

MOCENIGO

Hold him a moment.

[BORTOLO *exits.*]

Prior, my respects.
And though you do not ask it, Tintoretto
Will have your fresco in a twelvemonth.

PRIOR GABRIELLI

And the Pope, my prelude sooner.

MOCENIGO

Bless me, Father.

[*He bows his head. The* PRIOR *signs his brow with his thumb.*]

PRIOR GABRIELLI

May the blessing of the Lord Omnipotent
Descend upon you and remain forever.

MOCENIGO

Amen!. . . Bortolo! Present our guest!

[BORTOLO *enters and bows the guest into the room.*
  GIORDANO BRUNO *enters. He is a man of forty-three, more
ugly than handsome. He is dressed in a long, hooded cloak over
clothes which have seen better days. He is eager, cheerful, shrewd,
assertive. He is sensitive to slights, too apt to boast. He lacks
discretion and social subtlety.*]

BORTOLO

My lords,

The scholar, Giordano Bruno.

[Bruno *bows*.]

MOCENIGO
Welcome, sir!

BRUNO
What a night! Every road's a bog! Each lane
A cataract!

MOCENIGO
[*a note of distaste*]
This is the Prior Gabrielli,
Inquisitor General of the Serenissima!

BRUNO
[*cheerful*]
My honour! You are my first inquisitor!
The last, I hope!

[*The joke falls flat. The* PRIOR *studies* BRUNO, *groping for a recollection.*]

PRIOR GABRIELLI
Bruno . . . your given name?

BRUNO
My only one, sir.

PRIOR GABRIELLI
Where were you born?

BRUNO
                    Nola.

PRIOR GABRIELLI

I caught the accent of the South . . . an echo, too,
Out of our case-books. There was a certain friar
Of my own Order of Preachers, a fugitive
From vows, a vagabond philosopher.
He taught—now let me see—Paris and Oxford,
Prague and Wittenburg, Helmstedt and Zurich.
He was in prison there, I think. He wrote
An obscene comedy, some suspect treatises.
A work on memory, dialogues—his name . . .

BRUNO
[curt]

Giordano Bruno. I am he.

[*The* PRIOR *casts an inquiring glance at* MOCENIGO. *His silence is an irony.*]

PRIOR GABRIELLI
You are bold!
With your case open still, to put yourself
So close in reach of Rome and her pursuivants.

BRUNO

No, sir. I trust the justice of my cause,
The charity of Mother Church, the noble house
Which lends me patronage.

PRIOR GABRIELLI
You will remember,
You have no licence to teach publicly,
Nor preach in church nor give the sacraments.

17

BRUNO

I do not seek it, sir.

MOCENIGO

I am his surety.

[*The* PRIOR *bows and moves to the door with* MOCENIGO. *They ignore* BRUNO.]

Our bargain then is clear. You will write
With urgency to our high personage . . .

[*They exit.* BRUNO *slips off his cloak.* BORTOLO *takes it. He points to the sword-belt.* BRUNO *unbuckles it, chuckling.*]

BRUNO

Within these friendly walls, no further need.

[BORTOLO *exits.* BRUNO *relaxes, taking in his surroundings. He catches sight of the wine, pours himself a long draught and drinks with satisfaction. He sets down the glass and then begins to walk about the room, fingering its treasures. He is playing a comedy of self-mockery, the fortunate oaf who has found a feather bed. He pauses by an ornate mirror and jibes at his own reflection, sticking out his tongue, making faces as a child does.*]

BRUNO

Oh Brother Bruno! What a clod you are!
You talk, talk, talk, talk, talk!—
A very parakeet without the plumes.
You make jokes with the Grand Inquisitor,
Him with the thumbscrew in his pocket—bah!
I lose all patience with you—Raggedy Jack.

Empty of purse and belly, patched and darned,
Down to your last shoe leather—yet you strut
Like Socrates before he heard of hemlock!
Brother, little brother, mend your manners!
Tie your tongue! This is a dangerous city
For a babbler. Here they denounce you with a note
Unsigned, slipped in a lion's mouth, and then
One fine spring day, you're hanging by the heels
In the Piazza, dead as mutton!

[*There is a sound of voices outside. He composes himself instantly,
picks up a book from the table and assumes a studious pose.*
MOCENIGO *enters, with* BORTOLO *in attendance.* MOCENIGO
surveys his guest with ironic amusement.]

MOCENIGO

So! Master Bruno!

BRUNO

My lord?

MOCENIGO

You need new clothes!

BRUNO

[*wry*]

In truth I do!

MOCENIGO

A sober suiting, mind!

Scholarly, discreet. You bathe, I trust?

BRUNO

When I have money for the scrub-house, yes.

MOCENIGO

My steward pays your stipend by the month,
You may draw modestly against it. Are you poxed?

BRUNO

Not yet. The pox costs money, too.

MOCENIGO

No sickness of the lungs, infectious tumours?

BRUNO

None.

MOCENIGO

Do you drink?

BRUNO

Cheerfully.

MOCENIGO

No tavern brawls!
No tangles with the watch! The Mocenigo
Have a name to keep.

BRUNO

And I, my lord,
Have certain monkish ways to which I hold.

MOCENIGO

How much a monk, eh? I am tolerant
Of private peccadilloes, but I want
No swollen bellies on my servant-girls,
No sore-tailed pages in my retinue.
Play outside, eh?

[BRUNO *is silent.* MOCENIGO *is momentarily out of countenance.*
He goes on, more respectfully.]

> From first collation
> Until noon you are at call, and then
> From sunset until supper. If you walk abroad,
> My messengers must know how to recall you
> In an hour. You will tell no man—or woman—
> The secrets that we share. You do have secrets,
> Yes? Disciplines of power? Hidden arts?

BRUNO
[*grins*]
None that bear telling on an empty stomach.

[MOCENIGO *snaps his fingers at* BORTOLO.]

MOCENIGO
Bortolo! Supper for Master Bruno!

BORTOLO
My lord!

[BORTOLO *exits.* MOCENIGO *becomes eager and secretive.*]

MOCENIGO
Now, Master Bruno, let us say it plain.
You are a magician!

[BRUNO *laughs and dodges a direct answer.*]

BRUNO
You, my lord,

Have said it; but I do not admit the charge.
Why come to Venice to write my death warrant?

[MOCENIGO *laughs, too.*]

MOCENIGO
Well answered! But the Inquisitor is gone,
And we are secret here as hermits in a desert.
You have the formularies of the Jews?
You know the Cabbala? The secret names?
The invocations of Beelzebub,
The magic squares, the spells, the pentagram?
You practise alchemy? You can concoct
Love potions—and dispel the evil eye?

BRUNO
[*hedging*]
And if I could, my lord?

MOCENIGO
Make me an adept, too!

BRUNO
To what end?

MOCENIGO
To enrich yourself.

BRUNO
[*an irony*]
Such base
And mercenary use of the great powers
Entails a manifold damnation.

MOCENIGO
For me then!
Mocenigo is bent upon high enterprise.
Put power into his hands, and you have power
Beyond your dreaming. Be my tutor now
In magic arts and you will be my chamberlain,
Heart's favourite, beyond the touch of Rome,
The Ten, the whimsical malice of any man.
What say you, master?

[BRUNO *is now in a dilemma. If he confesses that he is not a* *magician,* MOCENIGO *may reject him. If he admits to magical* *power, he must make good the claim. He does not answer* *immediately. He hesitates, reflects and answers with sober* *conviction.*]

BRUNO
My lord, the things you ask,
I could engage to teach you. Give me vials,
Liquors and alembics, copper and lead,
A cellar to make the stinks in, I could be
The most proliferous alchemist in Europe.
But gold from lead? No man has done it, nor can.
Magic? Give me chalk and compasses,
A cat for my familiar, mouldy books
Written in a gibberish, I'll make the hairs stand up
On a clerk's tonsure! This is mummery
And humbug!

[MOCENIGO *now begins to show resentment and suspicion. He* *takes his jewelled dagger from its sheath and begins to whet the* *blade upon his thumb. His tone is sullen and insulting.*]

MOCENIGO
I am told otherwise by your betters!

BRUNO
[*snaps back*]
Betters or no, these are carnival tricks
For knaves to practise, fools to tremble at.

MOCENIGO
[*anger*]
Tell me straight. Can you make incantations,
Spells?

BRUNO
I can! And so can you!

MOCENIGO
How?

BRUNO
Walk
In town, look solemn, puffed with portents! Start
A whisper about any man—premise his death,
A looseness in his wife, a treachery
Of friends. Within a day, he's cringing from the prick
Of unseen daggers, fasting for fear of poison,
Slack as a string in bed! What else is magic
But play upon stretched nerves and hidden fears?
Love potions? Half a ducat buys enough
Cantharides to make a eunuch stand
Like a maypole, itch the crotch of every nun
From here to Padova. Mix it with bat's blood, newt's eye,
Nutmeg powder—what's the difference?

[Mocenigo *approaches him. There is the hint of madness in his face. He presses the dagger-point to* Bruno's *breast.*]

MOCENIGO

So tell me, Master Bruno. On your life
—This shabby and uncertain little span!—
Why should I feed you, clothe you, keep you safe
From the white hounds of God, pay you good gold,
To teach me what I know already?

[Bruno *is very cool. He has to be.*]

BRUNO

                    You should not!
Nor should you blame me, sir, because I will not cheat
To save my shabby self.

MOCENIGO
[*uncertain now*]
                    What have you then
For me, who pay the score?

BRUNO
[*blunt*]
                    A lifetime's learning!
Little or much, it's all the wealth I own . . .

[Bortolo *enters, carrying a supper tray. He sets it down on the table.*]

BORTOLO

The scholar's supper!

[MOCENIGO *relaxes and sheathes his dagger. His smile is a threat.*]

MOCENIGO
You are snappish, sir!
I hope to find you blander in the morning.
Good appetite!

[MOCENIGO *exits.* BRUNO *looks after him, frowning. Then he shrugs and turns to the meal. He does not sit, but inspects the meagre fare with distaste.*]

BRUNO
This is supper?

BORTOLO
[*veiled insult*]
                                        Have you
Eaten better?

BRUNO
[*anger*]
And in nobler houses!

[*He takes* BORTOLO *by the neck and forces him into the chair. He pushes his face down into the platter.*]

BRUNO
Go on! Look at it, man! Taste it! Smell it!
Corpse-cold! Too rank even for a beggar's belly.
Did your master order this? Or did you dream it
As a love-feast for Brother Bruno? Answer me!

26

BORTOLO

I—I carried what was served—

[BRUNO *hoists him to his feet and thrusts the tray into his hands.*]

BRUNO

                                        Then carry it back!
Tell them in the kitchen, I will eat
A bowl of soup, a roast of chicken, cheese,
A pear with grapes. —And send me honest wine,
Not vinegar.

BORTOLO

        I will order it.

[BRUNO *will not let him go, but twists his ear between thumb
and forefinger.* BORTOLO *writhes unhappily.*]

BRUNO

Bortolo?

BORTOLO

Sir?

BRUNO

A scholar is no butt for oafs.

BORTOLO

No, sir.

BRUNO

He comes to teach your master wisdom.

BORTOLO

Yes, sir.

BRUNO

And you a mannerly service!

BORTOLO

Yes, sir.

BRUNO

You will not keep me standing while you stuff
Your own belly in the kitchen, will you?

BORTOLO

No, sir.

My oath on that!

BRUNO

Swear for the cook, too.

BORTOLO

I swear.

BRUNO

And for the scullery maids.

BORTOLO

I swear!

BRUNO

I am hungry. Go!

[BRUNO *releases him and he trots out dolefully.* BRUNO *chuckles.*

He pours wine from MOCENIGO'S *flagon and carries it over to the casement. He draws back the curtains and throws open the window. The summer storm is over; there is moonlight and the sound of distant singing over the renewed rumour of the city.* BRUNO *sits in the alcove and relaxes into weariness.*

DONA DARIA *enters. She is a sad but stately beauty in her late twenties. She is carrying a book. She catches sight of* BRUNO, *who is absorbed in the outside spectacle. Her first greeting is cool.*]

DONA DARIA
Are you the scholar?

[BRUNO *is startled. He turns and gets awkwardly to his feet.*]

BRUNO
My lady?

DONA DARIA
Are you the scholar Bruno?

BRUNO
Yes.

DONA DARIA
I am the wife of Mocenigo.

BRUNO
[*bows*]
Madam.

DONA DARIA
You are not welcome here!

29

BRUNO

So I have found, my lady.

DONA DARIA
[taken aback]
                        My husband says
You are a notable heretic, a master
Of black arts.

BRUNO

Neither, madam.

DONA DARIA
                        My husband—

BRUNO
[grins]
Hoped for a trout, my lady, caught a catfish,
And is less pleased than you to have me here.

DONA DARIA

Why stay, then? Have you no pride?

BRUNO
                                Oh, pride a plenty!
But no money. Therefore no liberty,
Except to starve or—cheerful thought—to sell
Myself as galley rower at the docks.
Even for that I lack the muscle!

DONA DARIA
                                How comes
A man of brains to such a sorry pass?

BRUNO

Good question, madam! Why are we what we are?
I've gnawed at that dry bone for twenty years,
There's no meat left on it. The Mussulman
Comes closest to the answer. Our destiny
Is written on our palms; a bawdy joke,
The graffito of God we lack the wit
To read.

DONA DARIA
That is a blasphemy!

BRUNO
[exasperated]
Is it?
Then read my hand and make a psalm instead!

[There is a moment of silence as she stares at his out-thrust hand,
and then at his tight, angry face. Into the silence comes a song from
a young male voice outside the window. DONA DARIA softens.]

DONA DARIA
I beg your pardon, sir. I have no right
To plague you.

BRUNO
[relaxes]
I plague myself. Pebble-in-shoe,
Burrs-in-breeches Bruno!
[he adverts to the music]
What does he sing?

DONA DARIA
[*follows beat*]
"Farfalla, farfalla, farfalla vagante
Leggera sei tu come la mia amante."
The butterfly song—it tells of fickle love!

BRUNO
[*nostalgic irony*]
Fickle or not, it would be sweet to taste . . .

DONA DARIA
And has the scholar Bruno never loved?

BRUNO
I have been merry with women, sad betimes,
And solitary always in the morning.

DONA DARIA
Never a mistress?

BRUNO
Oh, yes!

DONA DARIA
Was she not kind?

BRUNO
Most cruel! Capricious as a folly-fire,
Cold and secret as a Pharoah's tomb,
Then of a sudden—Hey! Ho! Halloo!
A beat in the blood, a madness in the brain!

DONA DARIA
Where is she now?

BRUNO
Who knows?

DONA DARIA
What is her name?

BRUNO
Veritas . . .

DONA DARIA
The truth? You mock me, sir.

BRUNO
No, madam! There are a few of us—madmen all!—
Who are in love with knowing, who would sell
The last shirt from our backs for one small truth,
One tiny star-fire to light up the murk
And mystery of what we call our life . . .
We may go blind before we see it, that's
The haunting—

[*His mood changes as* BORTOLO *enters with the new supper tray.*]

Ah! Our ancient Ganymede!

[*He makes a comical inspection of the tray.*]

Much better! A scholar's compliment to all
Those sweating scullions. A platter for my lady?

DONA DARIA
No! This is my fasting day.

[BORTOLO *sets down the tray, pours wine and stands waiting.* BRUNO *seats himself ceremoniously, then waves* BORTOLO *away.*]

BRUNO
Go, friend, and sup
In peace and charity.

[BORTOLO *exits.* BRUNO *picks up a chicken leg and studies it.*]

A grace, madam.
—For the unwelcome guest?

DONA DARIA
I bid you welcome!
In the sweet name of God and in my own.

BRUNO
[*sober*]
I am thankful . . .

DONA DARIA
And hungry! Eat, sir, and enjoy!

[BRUNO *begins to eat ravenously.* DONA DARIA *relaxes and seats herself at the table.* BRUNO *talks between mouthfuls.*]

BRUNO
Why do you fast, my lady?

DONA DARIA
A discipline!

BRUNO
[*a note of mockery*]
Hairshirt as well? Cold vigils? Knotted cords?

DONA DARIA
[*sharp*]
And if there were?

BRUNO
Why so misuse what God
Has so munificently made?

DONA DARIA
Penance
Is enjoined upon us all. A monk
Should know that; even—

[*She breaks off.* BRUNO *completes the thought.*]

BRUNO
[*chuckles*]
Such a monk as I?
Madam, beware of celibates who first
Renounce, and then desire, and then, for shame,
Most rigorously condemn what they do not
Enjoy. This is a eunuch breed. For me,
God made woman a cushion for the world,
Her lips a honeycomb, her breasts a spring
Of sweetness, her hands a healing miracle,
Her womb a harbourage of fragile life
—Why would he then pronounce sentence of torment
On his masterwork?

35

DONA DARIA
[*a poignant revelation*]
He did it, Bruno,
Does it every day. The honeycomb
Is empty and the spring dried up. The womb
Is barren, nothing moves therein. No life,
No giver of life, only a nightly hunger
That must be stilled before it turns to frenzy.

[BRUNO *pours wine and offers it to her with bread and cheese. He is very gentle now.*]

BRUNO
Drink a little wine. Take this and eat.

DONA DARIA
[*puzzled*]
Why do you tempt me?

BRUNO
It was the last commandment
Of our Lord. Break bread in charity,
Two or three together. We are two,
It is enough to make an agape!

[DONA DARIA *begins to eat hesitantly, and then with enjoyment.* BRUNO *goes on with his meal.*]

DONA DARIA
Why do they call you heretic?

BRUNO
Beh!

They need a cry to rally up the hounds
And set them baying after Brother Fox!

DONA DARIA
That's half an answer—

BRUNO
                    And the other half,
How stand I, measured by the creeds, tradition,
The writings of the Fathers, acts of all
The councils, Nice, Chalcedon, Trent?
I do not know. I do not greatly care.
No man—prince, peasant, pope—has all the light,
Who says else is a mountebank. I claim
No private lien on the truth, only
A liberty to seek it, prove it in debate,
And to be wrong a thousand times to reach
A single rightness. It is that liberty
They fear. They want us driven to God like sheep,
Not running to him like lovers, shouting joy!

DONA DARIA
But why?

BRUNO
            Ever since the Greeks, we have been drunk
With language! We have made a cage of words
And shoved our God inside, as boys confine
A cricket or a locust, to make him sing
A private song! And look what great gob-stopping
Words we use for God's simplicity,
Hypostasis and homoousion!

We burn men for these words—a baboon chatter
Of human ignorance! —We burn men!

DONA DARIA

For their purpose then, it is enough
To have you heretic. Why are you called
Magician?

BRUNO

      They need hobgoblins, too—a fear
To hold the hunt together, so they eat,
Drink, sleep and breed, a single tribe,
Protective of itself, self-justified.

DONA DARIA

But are you not afraid?

BRUNO

      Oh yes, I am!
I am Red Reynard, broken-winded, torn,
Run down to rib-cage, scuttling to earth,
To lick his wounds, and get his courage up.

DONA DARIA

For what?

BRUNO

Another journey.

DONA DARIA
Where?

BRUNO
      Home!

DONA DARIA

And where is home?

BRUNO

      Oh, where is home? My lady,
You will laugh at my simplicity.
The quaint religion of a runaway.
Home is a convent, high on a Nolan hill,
Grey walls, a tired campanile that leans
Against blue sky, a cloister with white doves,
And orange-flowers and a sound of bells,
Vineyards that climb around the slopes,
Green fields, abundant in the summer sun,
The brethren picking beans and topping lettuces,
Skirts tucked into their cinctures, tonsures bare,
While the cicadas chant the matin song
Of Brother Sun!

[*He breaks off, caught in reverie.* DONA DARIA *prompts him
gently.*]

DONA DARIA

And what of Brother Bruno?

BRUNO

He comes, flip-flop in sandals, up the road.
He's slow, stooped in the back, his footsoles ache,
He's older by a century than when
He walked out, whistling, to confront the world.
The brethren wait. They have been pilgrims, too.
They have a patience for the wanderer,
They know the grail-search must be made alone.
They will not chide the prodigal, nor question him,
Enough that he is home . . .

[*He lapses again, and then abruptly shatters the self-created illusion.*]

                              O God! What home?
What brethren? I am a leper with a bell
Around my neck! Because I cannot bend
To all their systems and their syllogisms!

[*He slams a fist on the table, heaves himself up and strides to the window, where he stands, tense and rigid, staring out at the traffic of the Grand Canal.* DONA DARIA *stands, too, moves a pace or two towards him, and then stops. She is now what* BRUNO *has named her, the cushion of the world.*]

                    DONA DARIA
Master Bruno!

                    BRUNO
         Yes?

                    DONA DARIA
                    I am no judge of men.
I know—and him not well or happily—
Only the one I married. You are strange,
You take away the props that hold my faith.
You leave me shaken in a winter wind.
And yet . . .

                    BRUNO
                    [*harsh*]
         Ignore me, madam! I am a lackey
Here!

[*Unseen by both, unnoticed by the audience,* MOCENIGO *enters and stands in the gallery above.*]

DONA DARIA
Yet, in a city full of pigs,
You stand up like a man!

MOCENIGO
Bravissimo!

[*They both turn, shocked and speechless.* MOCENIGO *surveys them from above, like a puppet-master.*]

MOCENIGO
A noble vindication! Master Bruno,
You must have a care to earn the praise
My wife bestows on you. —And you, dear lady,
Will you come to bed and try your best—
Your very little best!—to make me, too,
Stand like a man!

[*There is a frozen moment and then* DONA DARIA *moves like an automaton up the stairs towards her husband.*]

[*Curtain*]

Scene II

[The same, 1592. It is still winter in Venice. A log fire blazes in the hearth. The drapes are drawn. Candles are lit.

*   Bortolo ushers in two visitors, Prior Gabrielli and Ludovico Taverna, the Papal Nuncio. Both are cloaked and hooded against the cold. Prior Gabrielli coughs asthmatically and talks compulsively.]*

PRIOR GABRIELLI
This fog!
A cobweb in the lungs! My bones protest
Each God-forgotten winter on the lagoons!

[They take off their cloaks and hand them to Bortolo.]

BORTOLO
My master begs your patience, gentlemen.

[Taverna chuckles and backs up gratefully to the fire.]

TAVERNA
Patience! Mine is worn thin around the backside!
Spavined nags, cold comfort at the inns,

Slush in the plains and snow in every pass
From Rome to the Romagna! His Holiness
Owes me a favour for this purgatory!

[BORTOLO *exits.*]

PRIOR GABRIELLI
Good news from Venice and he may double it.

TAVERNA
Have we good news?

[PRIOR GABRIELLI *makes a cautious gesture and drops his voice.*]

PRIOR GABRIELLI
Good dispositions here.
But problems to be solved. Mocenigo
Is ranged with Rome in secret, but must make,
For polity, a Venetian masquerade.

TAVERNA
That's a noble Christian!

PRIOR GABRIELLI
[*wry shrug*]
Our proverb says,
"Venetians first and Christians afterwards!"

TAVERNA
I did not come, Sir Prior, to peddle proverbs!
A new pontiff sits on Peter's throne,
Christ's vicar and my noble master Clement,
Eighth of the name. His charge to me is this:

"Find me a man who will hold Venice safe
Against the heretics, restore the old
Authority of Rome, the true respect,
For Christ, His vicar, and his hierarchy.
Find me that man, and pledge him our support,
Our Apostolic love, our princely might
Against the Church's enemies, and his!"
In Mocenigo, have we found him? Yes—
Or no?

PRIOR GABRIELLI
As far as I can read him, yes!

TAVERNA
How far is that?

PRIOR GABRIELLI
[*a studious care*]
Your Excellency knows
Better than I how power changes men.
Ask me to guarantee against the change
—I cannot. Nor can you. We ask and get
A promise of performance, A and B
And C and D, down to the final Zeta.
Then we say, "For our security
And the good faith of Mocenigo, seal
The bargain with a warranty!" Can we
Do more? What do we risk?

TAVERNA
A treachery!

PRIOR GABRIELLI
And if we do not risk? Venice is still

The Adriatic whore who'll sell herself
To English Protestant, Hussite or Zwinglian
—Yes, to a Muslim pirate—for their trade.

[TAVERNA *is still digesting this proposition when* MOCENIGO,
accompanied by DONA DARIA, *enters from the gallery. He is
cheerful and expansive.*]

MOCENIGO
Forgive me, sirs! My lady held me late
With a momentous matter, a seemly gown,
A modesty of jewels in which to greet
The legate of His Holiness . . .

TAVERNA
My lady!
From the hand of Peter, a benediction,
From myself, a humble greeting.

DONA DARIA
[*curtsies*]
Sir!
My thanks.

MOCENIGO
My house is yours. My life in service
To the Holy See. Wine for our guests!

[*They seat themselves as* DONA DARIA *pours wine.* MOCENIGO
talks on.]

Be comfortable! Firelight, fellowship,
And private talk. No protocol! No hedge
To what we say inside these walls! Your health!

[*They drink.* DONA DARIA *takes a book and retires discreetly to the alcove.*]

PRIOR GABRIELLI
My lord, the prelude has been played, and now
The curtain's up, the opera begins!

MOCENIGO
[*cheerfully*]
Sing it to me, Prior! My ear is good.
I promise not to miss a single grace-note,
Glissando or cadenza.

PRIOR GABRIELLI
So! We treat
Of sacred things, not politics!

MOCENIGO
Of course!

PRIOR GABRIELLI
Our noble pontiff, recently installed,
Weeps nightly at the rifts in Christendom.

MOCENIGO
And we weep with him.

PRIOR GABRIELLI
But not all. In Venice
In the sacred shadow of Saint Mark,
Lion of the Evangelists, we flirt
With schism. Our Senate names our bishops, not
The Pope! Our Patriarch—God give him light!—

Cannot convene a synod, unless the Doge
First nods approval! We ballot for our priests
Like prizes in a lottery. We exclude
All but Venetian born—so that if Paul
Or Luke or Mark came back as ministers,
We must refuse them. In this the Most Serene
And Catholic Republic, we are worse
Than English heretics, who make their King
—Their Queen, indeed!—a Pope. It must be changed!
The family of Christians must be one,
United in its Father's house!

MOCENIGO
[*irony*]
And I
Can bring them home?

TAVERNA
At least bring Venice back,
Out of Byzantium into the West.

[MOCENIGO *is too shrewd to be trapped into a facile promise. He
smiles and shakes his head.*]

MOCENIGO
My friend—believe me, I am more a friend
Than most in this fair city!—you must not ask
Impossibles! I must not claim to be
A thaumaturge who can make mountains walk!
How long was Rome a-building? Venice will not
Be made a virtuous woman overnight!

TAVERNA
How long, then?

MOCENIGO
       How long to come to power? How long
To use the power—fit lever under stone
And set it rolling?

TAVERNA
Guess, then!

MOCENIGO
       I will not!
Rather, I will show you—a risk to me,
But nonetheless an honesty I owe!—
What holds us anchored in Byzantium,
What makes our nobles jealous of privilege,
Our commons fractious, apt for novelty!

TAVERNA
[reluctant admiration]
You play boldly, sir.

MOCENIGO
       The stakes are high,
No less for Rome than me!

[He stands, dominating them. He is forceful and eloquent.]

       Let us be blunt.
Forget the reverent hypocrisies!
Remember Cambrai and the infamous league
Of French and Spaniards and Hungarians,
Led by Pope Julius—our spiritual father!—
To destroy our Most Serene Republic!
We are mistrustful now! With reason! We ask,

Do shepherds kill their sheep? Fathers their sons?
I stand in our Great Council and I plead
A catholic amity, familial love!
They laugh me out of countenance! I beg
A unity in faith, a resignation
Of old privilege. They wag wise heads
And tell me, "Who goes to supper with the Pope
Takes a long spoon and keeps his sword arm free!"
You know this, Prior. Your noble master, sir,
Carries Pope Julius on his back, dead
Though he be!

TAVERNA
            He wants to get him off!
He needs an advocate.

MOCENIGO
            The advocate
Needs time and subtlety, strong argument,
To make his case. Not in the Council only,
But with the people! They are restive now.
They know what Luther did in Germany,
They know that Rome is not impregnable,
That her decrees are not—not always, sir!—
Dictated by the Holy Spirit. So,
There is for us a double jeopardy,
The nobles and the commons!

TAVERNA
                  The commons are sheep!
They can be led or driven!

MOCENIGO
            Can they so?

49

[*At this moment* BRUNO'S *voice is heard, singing, a little drunk-enly, "Farfalla, farfalla." All turn at the sound. The* PRIOR *frowns,* DONA DARIA *looks worried.* MOCENIGO, *however, seizes the interruption to make his point.*]

Here's my Bruno! Here is a man who knows
The people in their habits and habitats.
He is common born, less than discreet,
Uncommon studious, with a lively ear,
A loose tongue, a taste for disputation.
Let us hear him!

PRIOR GABRIELLI
I beg you, no, my lord.
These are high matters—

TAVERNA
Let us hear him, Prior!

[BRUNO *enters, still singing, and then breaks off in tipsy surprise.*]

BRUNO
My lords! My lady! Forgive me! I have been
Abroad—no, not abroad. Settled felic—
Felicitously in a tavern, a place
For sailors on the Giudecca. There was a man,
A giant blackamoor, built like a barrel,
Baubles in his ears, a parrot red and green
Perched on his shoulder—a most eloquent bird!
Blasphemous, too! Spoke Greek and Arabic,
Italian and High German. This blackamoor—

[DONA DARIA *approaches and tries to draw him away.*]

DONA DARIA

Master Bruno, my husband and these gentlemen
Discuss affairs of state . . .

BRUNO

Oh! Then I'll go drink
A bowl of broth . . .

MOCENIGO

No! No! Sit with us!
We need a scholar's perspicacity.
More wine, good wife! A cup for Master Bruno.

BRUNO

You do me honour, sir.

[BRUNO *seats himself a little uncertainly under the disapproving*
gaze of the PRIOR. DONA DARIA *refills their glasses and offers a*
cup to BRUNO. *She hesitates a moment, and then retires to her*
window seat. BRUNO *sniffs the wine.*]

A better vintage
Than the tavern-lees. Your health, good sirs!

[*He drinks alone and then waits uncertainly.*]

MOCENIGO

Master Bruno, you have travelled much.

BRUNO

I am, sir, the most practised gallivant!

MOCENIGO

You have met high and low upon your journeys.

BRUNO

[*flattered*]

I have been lector to the King of France,
I have disputed in Oxford, I am friend
To learned lords in England—yet in truth,
I have lived lowly, too—with poxy sailors
And their trulls, horse-traders, pedlars,
Wandering charlatans . . .

MOCENIGO

So, tell us, Bruno

—There is rebellion in the air and schism
And heresy—what moves the common folk
Here in Venice, there in Wittenberg?

[BRUNO, *still tipsy, but touched at a tender point, weighs the question, and then answers it with gradually increasing eloquence.*]

BRUNO

What moves them? Beh! Hunger will make a riot.
Yet, hand out bread and onions, it will die
By sunrise. Lust? That's a disturber, too.
I saw today a fellow cut from breast
To belly-button for a tavern girl—
But when you talk rebellion, heresy
And deep disorders—ah! That's another tale!

TAVERNA

[*sharp interest*]

Tell it, Master Bruno. We who sit
Upon the powder-keg would like to know
What lights the fuse!

BRUNO
[*eager*]
Light! That's the word!
The abracadabra spell that springs the door
Into tomorrow. The light comes slowly, but—
By God!—it comes, to clown and chimney-sweep
And plodding serf.

PRIOR GABRIELLI
I do not understand.
Is this some new and specious revelation?

BRUNO
New to them. —But specious, no! Look!
On my master's book-shelves, there are maps
Which show the world is flat and that it ends
Just past the Pillars of Hercules, where flames
And horrid beasts devour lost sailor-men.
—There are no beasts! There are the golden lands
Cristoforo Colombo found, the Indies
And the seaways to Cathay! That's light!
Then there's Copernicus, and after him
—Who knows?—an infinite universe of suns,
And moons and undiscovered earths!

PRIOR GABRIELLI
[*snorts*]
Seductive novelties!

BRUNO
But, Prior, they wake
Men's minds to questioning. Who drew the dragons
On the maps? Cartographers or quacks?

Who says the Pope sees all creation plain
An hour after they have elected him?
Who says a king rules by God-given right?
There is no king in Venice. Does God dispense
One right in Spain, another, different, here?
The people ask, Prior! Their questions make
The groundswell, and the tidal wave comes after.

PRIOR GABRIELLI

This is sedition!

[DONA DARIA *gets up and moves towards the group.*]

BRUNO
                    To ask a question? Come!
If God be God and man a creature made
In image of the divine intelligence,
His noblest function is the search for truth.

PRIOR GABRIELLI
The truth is on deposit in the world,
Set there by Christ, interpreted by those
Who are his lawful delegates. You, sir,
Talk sophistry! You . . .

[DONA DARIA *intervenes, gently, but firmly.*]

DONA DARIA
                    Good Prior, our scholar
Did but answer truthfully a question
Set by my husband. We may disagree,
But not insult his probity.

PRIOR GABRIELLI
                    Madam,
I am reproved.

[BRUNO *gets up.*]

BRUNO
I beg to be excused.

MOCENIGO
I recommend the broth. Good wife, attend
Our scholar's needs!

[DONA DARIA *takes* BRUNO'S *arm and leads him out.* MOCENIGO
throws back his head and laughs.]

MOCENIGO
So there you have it, friends!
The truth, spoken in wine!

TAVERNA
More than that!
I am with the Prior. You harbour here
Sedition and a rabble-rousing rogue
To sell it in the streets!

MOCENIGO
[*cold and dangerous*]
Should you not ask,
As a discreet and careful emissary,
Seeking friends, the wherefore and the why?

TAVERNA
[*relaxes apologetically*]
I should. I do. I am saddle-sore
And sleepless. I beg you, grant me absolution
For bad manners.

PRIOR GABRIELLI
[*placating*]
We have a common care,
A common purpose.

MOCENIGO
A mutual trust, I hope?

TAVERNA
We have.

MOCENIGO
Good!

[*He gets up, crosses to a bureau, unlocks it and brings out a sealed
document. He returns, holding it ostentatiously in his two hands.*]

This is our treaty, then.
Rome is for Mocenigo. I for Rome,
On promise to restore, when I am come
To power in the Republic, all the rights
Of Mother Church, to root out heresy
And those who, on whatever pretext, teach
Or publish it.

TAVERNA
And the warranty?

MOCENIGO
[*holds up document*]
This! —A denunciation, notarised,
Over the name and seal of Mocenigo,
Of one Giordano Bruno, fugitive monk

And heretic, whom for security,
Surveillance and recording of his crimes,
I have kept in my house.

[*He hands the document to the* PRIOR *and turns to* TAVERNA.]

You are witness
For His Holiness. The document
Is now delivered to the Inquisitor.

[*The* PRIOR *accepts the document. He is puzzled and surprised.
There is a long silence.* TAVERNA *breaks it.*]

TAVERNA
Prior—with much respect—you have a case
In hand. Go, set the wheels a-turning, eh?

PRIOR GABRIELLI
[*flustered*]
Immediately! My lords!

[*The* PRIOR *exits.*]

TAVERNA
Mocenigo,
Noble to noble, tell me something!

MOCENIGO
What?

TAVERNA
Why would you, who have no need of rank,
Money, respect or credit, sell a man?

MOCENIGO

Why? We have had a council—Trent!
Its decrees—and mark me when I say it!—
Cut Europe like a cheese. Henceforth we are
Catholics and non-believers. How long
Can such a perilous division last?
A hundred years? Five hundred? I shall be dead
Before the outcome. So I place a bet
On the short run. Europe, at the core,
Is Christian. Ergo, the Church must win. This Bruno?
—A pawn! It is expedient for one
To die to save a multitude. Objections?

TAVERNA

None. Just so we know the rules and play
The game accordingly. Let's dine!

MOCENIGO
                              And drink
A safer wine than Bruno's, eh?

[*They exit, laughing.* BORTOLO *enters and resets the room. He
extinguishes all the candles except one candelabrum which he sets
on the table. He gathers up the used glasses and goes out. A few
moments later* BRUNO *and* DONA DARIA *enter.* BRUNO *is sober
now and* DONA DARIA *is chiding him affectionately.*]

DONA DARIA
                              Bruno!
Bruno! I have never known a man
So lovable and so recalcitrant.
Why do you drink?

BRUNO
I am a toss-pot. Simple!

DONA DARIA
No! I find you sober, night after night
Worrying your texts; and then I see you,
Black devils on your back, beating your head
Bloody against invisible walls. Bruno,
I wish that I could hold you then, against
This breast of mine—which is not mine, but his
Who married me—and calm you into silence.
Your tongue will hang you yet.

BRUNO
I know.

DONA DARIA
They hate you.
And they harass you.

BRUNO
Harass me, yes!
But hate me? No, dear innocent, they need me!

DONA DARIA
Need you?

BRUNO
They do! Every sect and state
Needs enemies, else it will die of bloating
And prosperity. Our Mother Church
Needs such a one as I, whom she can take
And say, "Look, this is a heretic!

This is Antichrist!" Then—ah, then!—
Little by little bend him—never break!—
But bend, with soft persuasion,
Argument and loneliness
—That's the real racking, loneliness!—
To a confession of the Faith, free,
Willing, humble, full of sad remorse.
See what they have then! One to recant for all,
One stone to beat a million breasts
Into a penitent salvation. —My texts,
Where are they?

[DONA DARIA *goes to the bookshelves and picks out the tomes.*]

DONA DARIA
                    Here!

[*She lays the tomes on the table and opens them.*]

BRUNO
[*wondering*]
You know the pages!

DONA DARIA
                                        The words!
The very syllables . . . [*quotes*] "De Immenso,
A poem by Filippo Bruno, called
Giordano, Doctor of Philosophy,
In which he treats of false astronomy,
Of unity and of the infinite."
Now, praise your pupil!

BRUNO
[*grins*]
In another time,

Another body, a better estate than this,
Richer and wiser, I should have married her!

DONA DARIA
Marriage, my little monk, is just a contract,
Publicly endorsed. The afterward,
The living of it, the loving in it, ah!
That's the apple-core!

BRUNO
You are not loved?

DONA DARIA
No, and yet I love!

BRUNO
[lightly]
The remedy's
A loving lover.

DONA DARIA
No! I cannot split
My woman's self into a courtesan,
A wife, an acrobat for prickling boys
In bed!

BRUNO
I would not wish it on you. I would . . .

DONA DARIA
What? . . .

[BRUNO does not answer. He takes her hand and kisses it,
without passion, but with great tenderness.]

BRUNO
Go to bed, my lady. Leave me
To this sterility. But when you pray,
Give me a moment's memory.

[*He bends to his books.* DONA DARIA *waits, reluctant to go.*]

DONA DARIA
Bruno?

BRUNO
Yes?

DONA DARIA
Do you ever pray?

BRUNO
Sometimes.

DONA DARIA
How?

BRUNO
Go to bed.

DONA DARIA
Please pray with me.

BRUNO
Oh, God!
Why do you torment me?

DONA DARIA
Pray with me!

[For a long and agonising moment, BRUNO battles with himself; then, tight and unhappy, he pushes himself out of his chair.]

BRUNO

Come to the window!

[They both cross to the window. BRUNO parts the drapes and throws open the casement. Moonlight streams into the room. BRUNO gathers himself and strikes an attitude. He begins on a note of bitter irony and then slips unconsciously into a moving self-revelation.]

           The prayer of Giordano Bruno,
Penny philosopher and one-time priest,
Magician by repute and heretic
By imputation, fomenter of sedition,
Boozer, braggart, fraud, and merry-Andrew
Dancing his jig upon the mountain top,
Waiting for star-fire . . . O God, if God there be!
O Christ, if they did not kill you forever
On your Calvary! O mother of Christ,
Who saw what men could do to one who heard
An alien music! Bend to me, be tender.
I am blind and deaf and dumb. And yet,
I do see visions, shout a kind of praise,
Feel in my pulse apocalyptic drums.

[They are so absorbed in the prayer that they do not hear the measured approach of the guards.]

The visions may be false. I do not know.
The praise may be a blasphemy. Forgive it.
The drums—O God, you set my heart a-pounding!

Whisper, just once, "Be still. You are at home
And safe!"

[*At this moment,* BORTOLO *enters and behind him an* OFFICER
and four soldiers of the civil guard.]

OFFICER
Giordano Bruno!

[*They turn, shocked.*]

BRUNO
I am he!

OFFICER
By order of the Council of the Ten,
At the request of the Inquisitors
Of Holy Mother Church, you are arrested,
Ordered into custody!

[BRUNO *is very calm.*]

BRUNO
The charge?

OFFICER
None! Only the order of the Ten.

BRUNO
I have been denounced?

OFFICER
I do not know.

DONA DARIA
[*bursts out*]
Captain, you are guilty of a trespass.
This is my husband's house!

BRUNO
[*grim*]
Madam, I fear
Your husband's hand directs the puppet-show!

DONA DARIA
[*horror*]
No!

BRUNO
Bortolo, fetch my cloak!

[BORTOLO *hesitates and then goes reluctantly.*]

[*very gently*]
And you,
Dear lady, please—please go to bed!

[*She cannot make the move. She breaks and clings to him. He
stands very erect, holding her and facing his captors.*]

[*Curtain*]

ACT TWO

Scene I

[*Venice, 1592. The prison of the Doge's Palace.*

The set is a composite, on two levels. The lower level is BRUNO'S *cell, a dismal hole furnished with a pallet bed.* (*As an annex to the cell, there is an* inset *which, when lit, shows a torture-room and a torturer.*)

The upper level is the examination room, where BRUNO *confronts the tribunal of the Inquisition. Stone steps lead from the cell to the examination room. When the scene opens,* BRUNO, *dressed now in a shabby, monkish costume with a cowl, is being led by a guard from his cell to the examination room. The Inquisitors await him, seated at their table, with their books and documents ranged before them.*

The Inquisitors are PRIOR GABRIELLI, *presiding;* LUDOVICO TAVERNA, *the Papal Nuncio, on his right;* LAURENTIO PRIOLI, *the Patriarch of Venice, on his left. At one end of the table, a little apart, sits* TOMMASSO MOROSINI, *Assessor of the Republic of Venice. At the other end is the* RECORDER.

BRUNO'S *guard stands him before the tribunal. There is a long silence, broken by the* PRIOR.]

PRIOR GABRIELLI
[*formal*]
Filippo Giordano Bruno, sometimes called
The Nolan, Doctor of Philosophy,
Presbyter, Clerk regular of the order
Of Friars Preachers, you are summoned here
To answer or refute sundry and various
Denunciations, touching your published works,
Your lectures, your opinions, whether expressed
In private or in public.

[BRUNO *throws back his cowl and holds himself erect and strong.*]

BRUNO
Most Reverend,
Of what am I convicted?

PRIOR GABRIELLI
[*shocked*]
Convicted, sir?
Of nothing. Here we are concerned with truth.
We make an inquisition into charges
Laid against you.

BRUNO
By whom?

PRIOR GABRIELLI
You may not know.

BRUNO
Their credit, Prior, and credibility
Touch me most intimately—threaten my life.

How do I challenge men who have no name,
No face?

PRIOR GABRIELLI
We test them, sir, as we do you.

BRUNO
[*sharp*]
But I am here, my lords, a prisoner
While they go free. You prove them perjured liars,
I am still robbed of these my precious days
Of light and liberty. Is this a justice?

PRIOR GABRIELLI
It is the method of the law.

BRUNO
And I
Have no redress against this loaded law?

PRIOR GABRIELLI
None, sir. We are the servants of what exists,
Until a later wisdom changes it.
The Clerk will read the charges.

BRUNO
A moment, please.

PRIOR GABRIELLI
[*testy*]
Yes? What now?

BRUNO
My cell is damp. My food
A bite above starvation. I am racked
With a rheumatic swelling in every joint.
I beg the courtesy of a chair.

[*The* PRIOR *snaps his fingers at the* GUARD, *who brings a chair for* BRUNO. *He seats himself.*]

PRIOR GABRIELLI
[*to* RECORDER]
The charges.

[*The* RECORDER *picks up a document and begins to read formally.*]

RECORDER
The first denunciation charges thus:
"This Bruno said: the Eucharistic rite
—Bread changed to flesh and blood—is blasphemy!
The Mass is magic for the ignorant.
The Trinity—Three Persons in one God—
Is an impossibility. A virgin
Giving birth without a man to seed her
Is a fraud. The miracles of Christ
Were conjuring tricks. Men's souls migrate
To animals. The universe endures,
Eternal, infinite—a million suns,
Uncounted earths. The scholar further said:
All priests and friars are asses, selling straw
To other asses. The first Apostles taught
By preaching and good works; but now the Church
Converts by force and not by love. Man must

72

Use his own liberty to come to God.
Our Church corrupts itself and makes of God
An image of its own corruption. Then,
Concerning marriage and the marriage act,
The Nolan thus proclaimed: The Church doth sin
In making sins of what serves man so well
And pleasantly"—

[*There is a slight pause. The Inquisitors study* BRUNO.]

BRUNO
[*relaxes and laughs*]
That's quite a catalogue!

TAVERNA
Of vicious errors!

BRUNO
Too many for one man!

MOROSINI
[*an ironic languor*]
And written in anger, too. It tastes of gall,
Splenetic indigestion.

BRUNO
Thank you, my lord.
And may I add a gloss? This document
Contains a contradiction. First it says
I am a kind of atheist, who rejects
The sum and substance of the Faith. Then—
God help us, gentlemen!—in the same breath,
I plead an apostolic love, a need

To come to God in Christian liberty,
Reform within the assembly of the Faith.
What does he want, my nameless enemy?
To flip a ducat for a bet and have it
Fall head and tail at once?

PRIOLI
Then you deny
Every and all the statements in the charge?

BRUNO
No, Excellency. I deny the import
And conclusion of the whole. I claim
A malice and malversation of my words.
Look! You are three clerics, schoolmen, trained
In argument and disputation. So
You know how you were taught—by pro and contra.
One day you stand in the debate and say,
"There is no God!—refute me!" Another day
You take another stand. It is the method,
Honourable and approved, from Plato
To Aquinas. When you use it, Prior,
Are you a heretic? No more am I!
But any fool or knave, hearing you talk,
Could wrench it out of frame and burn you for it!

PRIOR GABRIELLI
[to RECORDER]
You will note that the accused does not
Deny the formal words ascribed to him.
He does deny the taint of heresy.
He claims a malice in the informant.

74

MOROSINI

                                    Note
As well the evident discrepancy
And contradiction in the document.

                    RECORDER
It is done.

                    MOROSINI
                  [*more cold*]
          Request on my behalf,
As spokesman for the Serenissima,
A new interrogation of the writer.

                    TAVERNA
I approve that.

                    PRIOLI
          And I.

               PRIOR GABRIELLI
               It shall be done.
               [*to* BRUNO]
Now, Master Bruno, with some justice you
Object anonymous testimony. We
Grant the objection. Will you grant to us
The right to stand upon two other grounds
—The public record of your life, the books,
Which bear your name upon the title-page?

                    BRUNO
I grant it yes, but on conditions.

TAVERNA
What!

BRUNO
That I may still interpret and explain
My own words and myself.

PRIOLI
Should they need

Interpretation?

BRUNO
[*stoutly*]
Always, Eminence!
You lift your skirts on the traghetto, you
Expose—saving your Grace—a pubic part.
A modest maid cries gross indecency!
You claim a simple need—to piss or burst.
The act still needs explaining!

PRIOLI
[*laughs*]
Granted!

BRUNO
Thank you.

[*The* PRIOR *takes time to consult his papers. Then, a very formidable lawyer, he begins his brief.*]

PRIOR GABRIELLI
We begin then with the man—Filippo
Bruno, born in fifteen forty-eight

At Nola, in Campania. Studied in Naples,
Logic, humanities and dialectic.

                    BRUNO
              [*succumbs to garrulity*]
Good teachers, too—the best!—Teofilo
Vairano, Vincenzo Colle il Sarnese.
I remember them with love.

                PRIOR GABRIELLI
                        At seventeen,
You became a novice in the convent
Of Saint Dominic. The record states
"An avid student, prodigious memory,
A captious tongue, a will not easily bent
To discipline."

                    BRUNO
                   [*grins*]
              Hold our youth against us,
Prior, we should all be gallows meat!

[*This brings a laugh from all except the* PRIOR. *He goes on, re-
lentlessly checking off the notes.*]

                PRIOR GABRIELLI
You took vows then—promised solemnly
To live in poverty, in chastity,
Obedient subjection to the Rule
Of our most holy Founder, yes?

                    BRUNO
I did.

PRIOR GABRIELLI
You were ordained a priest?

BRUNO
I was.

PRIOR GABRIELLI
[*rams the point home*]
And then you broke the vows. You fled the convent
And the priesthood. Yes or no?

BRUNO
Yes.

[*The* PRIOR *has scored his first point. He lets the tribunal digest
it for a moment.*]

MOROSINI
[*a sardonic probing*]
Why did you do it, Master Bruno?

BRUNO
Why?
That is old history, my lord. I'll try
To reconstruct it. You have never been
A monk?

MOROSINI
Never, thank God!

BRUNO
A monastery,
My lord, is like a very little world,

Shut in behind stone walls. There are few saints,
Some who live in simple rectitude,
And others who, within the Church or out,
Would sell their sisters for a pastry-cake.
In this little world, there are no women,
Only men, who, in despite of fasts
And penances and prayerful nights,
Grow rank with their own seed, and then, like bulls
Penned in a common pasture, vent their rage
On one another. I was first accused
Of an impiety. I would not wear
Medallions of the saints around my neck,
Clustered like Bacchus' grapes. I still preferred
The simple image of the Crucified. Another time,
I found a brother monk fumbling my papers,
Sniffing for heresy, like a pig for truffles!
I hid them from him—in a privy! Boh!
Guilt was presumed and I arraigned for trial,
By Master-General in Rome. I had
No answer to conspiracy. I fled!

TAVERNA
"The guilty fleeth when no man pursueth."
That's in the scripture!

BRUNO
[anger]
                Do not judge me, sir,
By tags and texts! True justice is dispensed
Far otherwise!

TAVERNA
You are insolent, sir.

BRUNO
[*savage*]
Sit here and feel the sword–blade on your neck!
Let me pelt you with scraps of Holy Writ.
See how you like it!

PRIOLI
We must control ourselves!
We are a court, and not a bear pit! Bruno,
This flight of yours does bear a colour of guilt.

BRUNO
I know it, Eminence.

PRIOLI
Had you then the wit
To face down your accusers and to trust
The loving–kindness of our Mother Church,
You might not now stand in such jeopardy.

BRUNO
Eminence, at twenty–five, a rebel
And afraid, our Mother Church was like
A giantess, neglectful of her brood,
Careless of all their miseries!

PRIOLI
She was
And is your mother.

BRUNO
I, her son, still find

Her breasts are dry, her hands are less than gentle.
May I stretch my aching joints?

PRIOLI
Be free!

[BRUNO *gets up awkwardly, flexing his cramped muscles.* PRIOLI
watches him with pity and adds a gentle word.]

We are not gaolers, but inquisitors,
Seeking a common truth.

TAVERNA
[*springs a trap*]
And, Brother Bruno,
This would be one truth! You went to Zurich
And became a Calvinist!

[BRUNO *is at bay again. This is his real enemy.*]

BRUNO
I did!

TAVERNA
A renegade! A chaser after false
And alien creeds!

BRUNO
No, sir! A puzzled soul
Trying now that, now this, to find a hat
That fits his bursting brainbox!

MOROSINI
And you found it?

BRUNO
[*a tired grin*]
No! This tetchy imp who rides my back
Forbade me such a peace. I quarrelled, sir,
With those Swiss sobersides and spent a time
In gaol!

TAVERNA
[*heavy irony*]
So! It seems, good Brother Bruno,
You are neither fish nor fowl. Among
The heretics you are the orthodox,
And with the faithful, more an atheist
Than Julian the Apostate.

BRUNO
[*quietly*]
Excellency,
Have you ever had a son?

TAVERNA
Never!

BRUNO
Nor I. But, if we had, would we not see
Him grope and strain from infancy to boyhood,
Boy to man, testing himself against
A strange, strange world? Would we not pity him
And stretch a father's hand to lift him up
From darkness into light?

TAVERNA
But, if and when
He comes to manhood, must we hold him safe
From all his follies?

BRUNO
If we love, we try.
[*a shrewd challenge*]
The Church is our common Mother, so I ask,
How do you see me, sirs? A son, a brother
—or an enemy?

TAVERNA
We do not know.
A heretic can have no part in Christ.
Or the Assembly of His Holy Ones.
[*he picks references out of his papers*]
We note, you see, in all your wanderings,
This curious circumstance—your patrons and
Your friends, in England, Germany and France,
Are all the rebel breed of Protestants.
Your lectures and your disputations, such
As were delated to us, all reject
The classic lines of Christian argument.
[*sarcasm*]
You must not blame us if we smell at least
A wolf under the sheepskin!

PRIOLI
[*hastily*]
In spite of that,
We wish to treat with you in charity.

BRUNO
All of you? You, Prior, Excellency, you?

MOROSINI
[*cool advice*]
Brother Bruno. Do not bet your life
Upon our Christianity. Convince us!

BRUNO
[*helpless shrug*]
How?

PRIOR GABRIELLI
Be seated, sir.

[BRUNO *wilts a little and seats himself.*]

                    Your books are you.
No argument?

BRUNO
No argument. Except—

TAVERNA
[*contempt*]
Always exceptions! Never an answer plain.

MOROSINI
[*ironic defence*]
The man is a philosopher! He needs
A definition of the terms!

84

TAVERNA
[*shrugs*]
So be it!

BRUNO
[*a curious, pleading note*]
Prior, like me, you are Dominican?

PRIOR GABRIELLI
Yes.

BRUNO
We learned the same theology.

PRIOR GABRIELLI
Yes.

BRUNO
Our masters said free speculation
Is allowed, on every matter but
The substance of the Faith. Do you agree?

PRIOR GABRIELLI
I do.

BRUNO
So, when I reason in my books
Of nature and the natural order—right
Or wrong—I am beyond attainder. Yes?

PRIOR GABRIELLI
[*dubious*]
Yes. But if you make one step beyond

The natural into the realm of Faith,
You fall under the law.

BRUNO
Whose law, Prior?
Before I piously consent to hang
Myself with this your codex, may we please
Examine and interpret it together?

TAVERNA
[*furious*]
My God! The man's a legal trickster.
Spinning a web of court-room sophistries,
Just to distract us!

BRUNO
Am I, Sir Nuncio?
[*he speaks now with a great and grave dignity*]
Let me show you what I am. One man
Without an advocate or single friend
In court. I have not slept too well because
Of damp and rats inside my cell.
I have not prepared my case. You—
Only you have seen the documents.
Besides, there is no candle in my cell
To read by. I face you—four judges and
A clerk! Behind you, what? The majesty
Of Venice and her Empire, the might of Rome,
And all the princes who support her, all
The army of the orthodox. Give me,
At least, the time to argue for my life.
—Or finish this base comedy, and burn me
Now!

[*He has silenced them for the moment. Out of the silence, a new man begins to emerge, slowly, from the* PRIOR. *He is not and will never be a hero. But he begins to walk a certain way up the mountain.*]

PRIOR GABRIELLI
Your point is taken, Brother. I
Do urge upon my colleagues to refrain
From harassing the accused and to respect
His right of argument. Bruno, you asked
A statement of the law. We put it thus.
Our Saviour, Jesus Christ, came down to earth,
God in human flesh, and gave us all
A revelation of eternal truth.
He left, to Peter and his successors,
The keys of Heaven, authority to preach,
Interpret and unfold the moral code
Implicit in the truth. That is the Right
Of Peter; the rest of us, bishops and priests,
May use the right, by lawful delegation
Only. Are you answered, Brother?

BRUNO
                    No!
I have to ask, because my liberty
Depends on it, who says with certainty
What is a matter of Faith, and what of proper
Speculation?

PRIOR GABRIELLI
The limits are defined
From time to time by Papal documents,
The councils and the Church's common mind.

BRUNO

But the limits change. So what may burn
Me now, tomorrow may make me saint and doctor
Of the Church. You see my problem! Christ
Had never heard of Transubstantiation.
I vote for Christ, I am baptized into
The Christian family. —Am I then cast out
For a new word Saint Paul might choke on!

TAVERNA

Do you reject the word?

BRUNO

I have not said so.

PRIOR GABRIELLI
[shrugs]

We can argue this into absurdity.
You asked a statement of the law. You have it.
Begin now with these books: "Of Infinite Worlds"
And "Of the Principal and Primal Cause."

[He holds up the volumes, displaying the title pages. He makes a lawyer's switch.]

A curious thing! The title pages say
"Printed in Venice." Were they not, in fact,
Issued in England?

BRUNO
[humbled]

Yes.

TAVERNA
Another lie!
A little one, but most significant.

BRUNO
[*lamely*]
My publishers advised it.

TAVERNA
You connived!

BRUNO
For better money. Yes!

TAVERNA
Does this not
Make you a venal man?

BRUNO
It does, perhaps,
But I was very poor.

[*It is another mark against him. The tribunal notes it silently.*]

PRIOR GABRIELLI
In these works
You state the Universe extends beyond
Our vision, to infinity. Our world is
One of many.

BRUNO
Yes.

89

PRIOR GABRIELLI

Are we not
At one stride into heresy? Is not
Infinity an attribute of God,
And only God?

BRUNO
[*eager*]
I say that God himself
Is co-extensive with his universe!

PRIOR GABRIELLI
[*riffles pages*]
You say more! "What we call the Creator
Is that which animates us all." Already
You are out of nature into Faith.
You are in conflict—

BRUNO
I—I did not mean it
Thus.

TAVERNA
But thus you wrote it. Your books, you said,
Are you!

[BRUNO *is silenced. The* PRIOR *presses his advantage. He gets
up and, carrying one of the volumes, goes to* BRUNO.]

PRIOR GABRIELLI
Now read the passage I have marked.

[BRUNO *takes the book and reads hesitantly.*]

BRUNO

"The soul, the anima, being a thrust
Of the Eternal Energy, continues
After one body's death, to animate
Another envelope, human or animal."

PRIOR GABRIELLI

Stop there!

[*He takes back the book and returns to his place at the table. He
is very grave and very clear, as befits a good advocate.*]

Brother Bruno, here we have
Two propositions. Both are yours, and both
On face of it—heretical. The Church
Has always taught that human souls do not
Migrate. That God, eternal, infinite,
Is infinitely greater than his own
Creation. Sustains it, but is separate!

PRIOLI
[*frowning*]
I am concerned. The statements correspond
With the first charges read.

TAVERNA
[*sour triumph*]
I think we'll find,
As we walk Brother Bruno down the road,
That the denunciation he objected
Is a true bill of particulars,
Written by an honest man—as shocked as we
By the opinions of this self-styled scholar.

What say you, Brother? Better confess it now,
Than stretch the patience and credulity
Of this tribunal!

[BRUNO's *reply is less certain than his others. He is shaken and tries to play for time.*]

BRUNO
                I will not confess.
I stand on my first claim—freedom to enquire,
Hold and express opinions on any subject
In the natural order. I further claim
Everything that I have written or said
Conforms in substance to the Deposit of Faith.
Give me paper, pens and ink, give me
My books, a copy of the bill against me,
Time—and some light within my cell—I'll prove
My orthodoxy, point by point. Errors
There may be, but of expression, not intent.
These I will happily recant and edit out
Of future printings.

TAVERNA
[*laughs contemptuously*]
                There's a serpentine
Concession! "I am absolutely right,
But if I am wrong, I'll change it overnight!"
This fellow will keep us here a twelvemonth
With his sleight of hand. Give him paper
Enough, he'll scribble us all into the grave!

MOROSINI
[*cool as ever*]
He has a right to answer, does he not?

He has a duty to recant when once
Convinced of error. He offers that. Why not
Accept?

TAVERNA
                    Because I do not trust him! He shifts
And changes like a weather cock! He is
A liar, self-confessed!

PRIOLI
                    In spite of that
We have a clear commission: sober study,
A dispassionate verdict, a sentence fit
For what misdeeds are proved, a merciful
Concern for the immortal soul of this
Our troubled brother.

TAVERNA
                    I say we execute
Our charge the better if we cut away
Confusion!

PRIOLI
                    How?

TAVERNA
[cold]
Put Bruno to the Question!

[*The demand shocks them all.* BRUNO *sits in mute horror. The*
PRIOR *grows a little larger.*]

PRIOR GABRIELLI
No! I will not consent!

TAVERNA
You will! You must.

PRIOR GABRIELLI
The intention of the law is clear. The court
Shall not put any man to torture who
Has not displayed obduracy and contempt.

PRIOLI
That is true.

TAVERNA
I say Giordano Bruno
Is a hardened, contumacious cheat.

MOROSINI
I disagree. He stands in peril here,
He may use any tactic in defence.

TAVERNA
The court being disagreed, then I invoke
Authority. Eminence, you are
The Patriarch of Venice.

PRIOLI
Yes.

TAVERNA
From whom
Did you receive your bishopric, your title?

PRIOLI
From the Pope. The vicar of Christ.

TAVERNA

Prior,
Who gives the Preaching Friars their brief, their high
Responsibility within the Church?

PRIOR GABRIELLI

Rome. His Holiness.

TAVERNA

This tribunal
Sits by his order?

PRIOLI

Yes, it does.

TAVERNA

And I,
As Papal Nuncio, here represent
That same high person Clement, by God's Grace,
Head of the Universal Church. With this
My patent, in the name of God, I say,
Giordano Bruno shall immediately
Be put to the Question.

[BRUNO *breaks and cries out.*]

BRUNO

You cannot do this!

TAVERNA

Be silent! Gentlemen, what say you all?

MOROSINI

A small reminder, Excellency!

TAVERNA
Yes?

MOROSINI
The instruments of death and torture are
At the disposal of the secular arm
And not the Church. Not here, in Venice, sir!

TAVERNA
You refuse me, then?

MOROSINI
[*smooth*]
Not yet. I wait upon
A formal and polite request from Rome
—Through you—to the Republic, which in this court
Is me!

[TAVERNA, *hating him, is forced to accept the diplomacy. He recovers himself and makes a very formal request.*]

TAVERNA
Messer Morosini! I request,
Formally and with profound respect,
Co-operation to complete the work
Of this most Holy Roman Inquisition!

MOROSINI
[*studious deliberation*]
To aid the Faith, and, further, to cement
The friendship of Rome and Venice—I consent.

PRIOR GABRIELLI
I register objection!

TAVERNA
[*contempt*]
Note it, Clerk!

[BRUNO *is on his feet, trembling.*]

BRUNO
You are horrible men! You have no pity!
You play a power game with human lives,
You crucify the Christ you say you love,
In us his helpless children.

TAVERNA
Take him, guards!

[*The guards take* BRUNO *out roughly. Instinctively the Inquisitors stand. The lights dim slowly in the examination room and come up bright in the lower cell, where a masked torturer waits amid his sinister array of instruments. Bruno is led to the rack and as the guards begin to strip him*

Black Out]

Scene II

[*The same. Night. Two lanterns hung on the wall throw a dim light on the examination room. A sleepy guard sits on a stool at the door of* BRUNO'S *cell. The cell is in darkness. Two figures, cloaked and hooded, enter the examination room. They are not immediately identifiable in the dim light, but one is* MOROSINI *and the other* DONA DARIA.

    The guard wakes up and stands to attention. MOROSINI *leads* DONA DARIA *to the table and seats her there. He approaches the guard. He indicates the door of the cell, but does not speak. The guard unlocks it. He takes a lantern from the wall and leads* MOROSINI *into the cell.*

    Now the examination room is very dim and the cell is illuminated.

    BRUNO, *wrapped in his cloak and covered by an old blanket, lies huddled on the pallet bed.*

    MOROSINI *and the guard stand looking down at him.* MOROSINI *waves the guard away. The guard sets down the lantern and exits, closing the door, but not locking it.* MOROSINI *pulls a wooden stool to the side of the bed and sits. He throws back his hood, revealing himself. He is still the ironic assessor.*]

MOROSINI
[*to the sleeping man*]
Poor little man!
So puffed up with your fine philosophies,

You cannot even read the weather signs!
The thunder's rolling round your ears, and you—
You are still listening for nightingales!

> [*he shakes* BRUNO]

Wake up! Wake up, Master Bruno!

[BRUNO *stirs, groaning into wakefulness. He has been racked.
Every move is a torment. His speech is spasmodic and painful.*]

BRUNO

No!
No more, I beg you! Who—who are you?

MOROSINI

A friend!

[*He holds the lantern up to his face.* BRUNO *recognises him and
lies back wearily.*]

BRUNO

Such friends! God save me from my foes!

MOROSINI

He cannot, being a prisoner like you
Of theologians and inquisitors!
I can, and will.

BRUNO

You! I remember now!
You sold me to the torturers—to aid
The Faith . . .

99

MOROSINI
[*amiably*]
Not sold! Just lent! To teach you, friend,
A necessary wisdom!

BRUNO
Give me water,
I am burning up!

[*There is a wooden pail and a ladle at hand.* MOROSINI *scoops up water and offers it.* BRUNO *cannot help himself.* MOROSINI *hoists him and holds the ladle to his lips. He drinks, chattery and greedy, slopping the liquid. He lies back, exhausted.*]

MOROSINI
Can you hear me?

BRUNO
Yes.

MOROSINI
And understand?

BRUNO
[*a relic of humour*]
I understand, my lord,
Only the believing's difficult!

MOROSINI
[*genuine admiration*]
I like you, Bruno. You are much a man!
But not enough—no man is ever enough

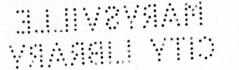

To beat the last turn of the rack, the last
Hot iron on the foot-soles.

BRUNO
Go away!

MOROSINI
Do you know who betrayed you?

BRUNO
          Mocenigo.

MOROSINI
More, my friend! Ciotto the bookseller,
Brother Celestine, the Capuchin,
Graziano the Neapolitan—
Those two were prison friends with whom you joked,
Shared bread and cocked a snook at piety.
—All of them told their little tales upstairs.
Volumes of petty treachery, enough
To burn a dozen Brunos!

BRUNO
         I am sick
Of this sick world!

MOROSINI
         They will not let you out
So easily. They will tread you, brother,
Like a grape, down to the pips and skin!
And the skin they'll nail up on the door
And say, "Look, this was an heresiarch!
Another Arius, another Luther!"

BRUNO

Heresiarch! My God, how do they dream
These calumnies!

MOROSINI

      They do not dream. They are
The most pragmatical of men. As I am.

BRUNO

What do you want?

MOROSINI

      To cheat the Mocenigo,
Spit in his shifty eye. Do you know yet,
My baby Socrates, why you were sold?

BRUNO

He wanted me to teach him magic. I
Could not. He thought I cheated him.

MOROSINI

O God! The innocence of scholars! Look!
You were a gift from heaven to Mocenigo!
He wants the favour of Rome. He thinks to buy it
With you, a bright new heretic!

BRUNO

      But you?

MOROSINI

I want you to confess, tomorrow. Sign
Whatever abjuration they dictate.

BRUNO

And then?

MOROSINI

Then you belong to Venice, not
To Rome. We sentence you. A modest term
Of penance, in a pleasant convent, where
The wine is good and books are plentiful.
When you're forgotten, in a year or two,
We'll give you gold, safe conduct and a horse,
And send you packing in to Germany!

BRUNO

[bitter]

I wish I could believe the half of it!

MOROSINI

Unless I can convince you, you are lost!

BRUNO

Give me a grain of hope!

MOROSINI

Better than that.

[He gets up, goes to the door of the cell, opens it, enters the examination room and beckons to DONA DARIA. She crosses to him,
still hooded and unrecognisable. She precedes him into the cell.

   She stands a moment looking down at BRUNO. In a single
movement, she kneels and throws back her hood. She is shaken
by the sight of his extremity.]

DONA DARIA

Master Bruno!

BRUNO

My lady!

[*He struggles to sit up, is cramped by a sudden pain and falls back, gasping.* DONA DARIA *turns to ask for help from* MOROSINI, *but he is already at the foot of the steps and closing the door. He crosses the examination room and takes the position she has left.*

DONA DARIA *throws off her cloak, opens her reticule and takes out a handkerchief, a vial of perfume and a small silver flask. She sprinkles perfume on the handkerchief and bathes his face with it.*]

DONA DARIA
[*anger*]
Thank God I have
No children, lest I mother men like these!

[BRUNO *raises a clawed hand to stroke her forehead. He is broken by weariness and relief.*]

BRUNO
You are the first light I have seen. My own
Small star. . . !

[DONA DARIA *takes his hand and studies it, horror-struck.*]

DONA DARIA
What have they done to you?

BRUNO
[*small grin*]
My lady,

They have a whole compendium of arts
To make us suffer.

[DONA DARIA *kisses the twisted hand, then holds it to her breast.*]

DONA DARIA
My husband laid the charges?

BRUNO
He and the others. There is so much hate—

DONA DARIA
I have my share of it to spend!

BRUNO
Hush! Hush!

[*he groans as a sudden pain takes him*]

Forgive me! I am torn with cramps and rigors!

[DONA DARIA *reaches for the flask and holds it to his lips.*]

DONA DARIA
Drink this! I had it from my apothecary,
A liquor and an opiate to ease
The pain.

[*He drinks and she settles him back.*]

BRUNO
How came you here?

DONA DARIA
[*bitter*]
                    I used to be
—Before I knew the terror of the Church—
A visitant of lazarets and prisons,
—Our Lady of the Sorrows, that's the name
We gave our little confraternity.
I saw our noble Patriarch. I begged
To visit you. He, piously, demurred,
Then handed me to Morosini, who,
Having no claim to piety, consented.
So, I am here.

BRUNO
          Morosini wants
My recantation.

DONA DARIA
[*eager*]
     So do I!

BRUNO
[*utter bewilderment*]
               Of all
The women in the world, not you!

DONA DARIA
[*very gentle*]
                    My love
—Yes, I can say it now, here, where there is

No love!—my love, my master in magic arts,
I have read all your books, dreamt all your dreams.
I tell you, not one of them is worth your life.

BRUNO

How can you say that?

DONA DARIA
[*deep loving pity*]
You are so much a monk,
My dear, dear friend, so much a cloud-walker,
You do not see the violets in the grass.
Give me your hands. I kiss them. Hands that wrote
Visions that have transported me. But, Bruno,
[*she presses his hands to her body*]
Let me feel here one stirring of new life,
One flush of milk into these breasts—and I
Renounce your visions for reality.
A life! A human life! Flesh and blood,
And that strange other thing, a human mind!
You are alive, my love. So let them burn
Every last book! You can write again!
Dead, they will scatter your ashes to the wind,
And who will hear the piping of your ghost
At midnight? Not even I.

BRUNO

I am so tired.

DONA DARIA

Good! The opiate is working.

BRUNO
                Why—
           [*a great effort*]
Why have you robbed me of my anger?

DONA DARIA
                                    To give
You back your life.

BRUNO
          [*fighting darkness*]
          It is not enough!
A man, to live a man, has to know when
To die.
               [*a last effort*]
     There must be reasons—reasons—!

[*He collapses.* DONA DARIA *soothes him like a child.*]

DONA DARIA
                              Sleep now!
My tired lover, who has never loved,
My stargazer whose constellations stand
Always in contradiction. Sleep. . .! Sleep!

[BRUNO *sleeps. She draws the blanket tenderly about him, puts
on the cloak and hood, picks up the lantern and mounts to the
examination room, as the guard locks the door. She crosses to*
MOROSINI, *who rises at her approach.*]

MOROSINI
Well, my lady? Will he bend to what
We plan for him?

DONA DARIA
I hope, I pray he will.
[*a sudden cold threat*]
I pray, sir, if he does, that you will keep
Your bargain!

MOROSINI
[*sincere*]
I will try.

DONA DARIA
No, sir! Not try!
Perform!
[*a terrible simplicity*]
I promise you, if you do not,
I will run mad in Venice, telling this tale,
Shouting your plots on the Rialto, crying
Your treachery in taverns, cuckolding
My noble husband, skirts up, hunkers down,
In every alley.

[*In a sudden, cold anger,* MOROSINI *takes hold of her.*]

MOROSINI
Understand me, sweet!
Cuckold your husband, pox him every night,
I'll send you diamonds! But breathe a word
Of these our strategies, I'll have you dead
Within a week, or bricked up in a cell
Beside a church!

DONA DARIA
Do not threaten me!

MOROSINI
[*relaxes a little*]
I make no threat. I tell you simple truth.
We are all beleaguered here. Rome
Is vowed to stamp out heresy, or else
Europe is split forever. Venice is pledged
To be the Most Serene Republic till
The dawn of doomsday. Your noble husband wants
The Doge's hat—or else new testicles!
You want your scholar safe. I want him free
To thwart this scheming Nuncio of ours
And put the evil eye on Mocenigo!
Where do we end? We play with tarot cards,
Who gets the hanging man? We do not know.
We pity him and let him die, because
We are all forest beasts who want to live!
Well, madam?

DONA DARIA
Take me home!

MOROSINI
[*ironic courtesy*]
                    Your servant,
Lady Mocenigo.

[*They exit.*]

[*Black Out*]

Scene III

[*The same. Morning. The tribunal is assembled. The guards are posted.* MOCENIGO *sits in the chair, under re-examination.*]

MOCENIGO
[*testy*]
I am troubled!
Three times I have presented to this court
My written depositions. Why am I now
Badgered with all these questions?

TAVERNA
[*smooth*]
                    Please, my lord,
Permit an explanation. We do not,
In Roman legal usage, imitate
The Germans who, with plea and counterplea,
Make a dispute for justice like a joust
Or tournament. We enquire, we delve,
Like miners chipping at the dross,
To find the single vein of gold—the truth.

MOCENIGO
[*cold*]
Does your Excellency suggest that I,
Over my hand and seal, compound untruth?

111

MOROSINI
Not his Excellency, but the accused.
He claimed—the record will confirm it—
"Malice and malversation."

MOCENIGO
He lies!

MOROSINI
[*smooth*]
Of course,
But we must prove he lies.

TAVERNA
[*a tart reminder*]
Because he stands
At risk—not you, my lord, who have discharged
A Christian duty, and whom we hold safe.

MOCENIGO
[*grudgingly mollified*]
Now that I understand . . .

PRIOR GABRIELLI
We ask you this:
The character of Bruno, how would you
Describe it?

MOCENIGO
[*studious moderation*]
Well, at first sight, agreeable!
Garrulous perhaps, but still a wit!
Quick-tempered, passionate in argument.

112

Sometimes, in his cups, he'll play buffoon,
But sober, he can be learned and profound.

MOROSINI
Not stupid?

MOCENIGO
Never! On the contrary,
Most devious and subtle.

MOROSINI
In the end,
You did not like him?

MOCENIGO
I mistrusted him.

MOROSINI
He knew that?

MOCENIGO
Yes. I am jack-blunt, I make
No secrets.

MOROSINI
Thank you. Please continue, Prior.

[*The* PRIOR *refers to his documents, then addresses* MOCENIGO.]

PRIOR GABRIELLI
Consider this part of your testimony:
"One day, while walking out with Bruno—I
Remember we were going to Saint George

113

The Greater for a Mass—he said these things:
'Christ was a sad fellow, who seduced
The people with his magus tricks. His friends
Were better men than he, because they died
Most willingly, while he feared death and tried
To flee it!' "

MOCENIGO
I remember that.

TAVERNA
It was
Plain heresy!

MOCENIGO
No less!

MOROSINI
[moves in for kill]
And yet the man,
Who spoke it—subtle, devious,
Knowing your rancour and mistrust—would put
A sword into your hands to kill him with.
Come, my friend!

MOCENIGO
I am insulted, sirs!

PRIOLI
[mildly]
Why so? Our learned colleague simply points
To certain contradictions, asking you
To make a true equation of the facts.

MOROSINI

Put it another way: which Bruno have we
In the cells? Yours? Or another man,
Quite different?

MOCENIGO
[*battling for composure*]
I do not understand
The import of the question.

MOROSINI
Slowly then,
We'll come to it. You know the little lane,
A minute from San Marco? The street of dolls—
The vulgar have another name for it!—
Where they make children's puppets and marionettes?
Well, they begin with wooden manikins,
No face, no eyes, just limbs and trunk and head,
Each one alike. Then they begin to paint.
Six strokes and there's a Harlequin! Presto!
Mouth up!—and there's a cheerful cavalier!
Mouth down!—and there's a sad old Pantaloon!
Your Bruno, sir—and we know ours right well,
We stood and watched him racked. We heard him scream—
Is but a painted man. You see our problem?—
You paint too perfectly—no living man
Can match your jumping doll, be he a saint
Or satanist!

[MOCENIGO, *trapped, looks round the faces of the court. They are all closed against him. He makes a desperate counter-attack.*]

MOCENIGO
You have conspired to bring
Me to this moment.

115

PRIOLI
[*his first real strength*]
No, sir! We have not
Conspired!

MOCENIGO
I was hasty, Eminence.
Forgive me!

PRIOLI
You are forgiven. You may go.

MOCENIGO
But, Eminence, my credit here? My name?
My reputation for integrity?

PRIOLI
Will have the weight which they deserve, when we
Deliver judgement! Sir, you are excused.

[MOCENIGO *takes one last look at the unfriendly faces and exits.*
MOROSINI *caps the exit with a sniper's shot at* TAVERNA.]

MOROSINI
There goes a man who thought to be a doge!
If ever he wore the cap—God help us all.

PRIOR GABRIELLI
[*to guard*]
Bring in the prisoner!

[*The guard unlocks the door and descends to get* BRUNO. *The Inquisitors rustle their papers and confer briefly, until the shock of*
BRUNO'S *entrance silences them. Physically, he is a twisted man.*

116

The guard has to support him. In spite of this, as he sits, he still manages a flash of the old humour.]

BRUNO

Excuse me my decrepitude, good sirs!
Your ministers below were overzealous!

[*They have the grace to be ashamed for the moment. The* PRIOR *makes another small show of strength.*]

PRIOR GABRIELLI
[*to guard*]

Bring cordial and a goblet. Set it by
His chair!

[*The guard goes out.*]

PRIOLI

Are you well enough to stand
A questioning?

BRUNO
[*quiet*]

I do not know. At least
I am less pained than on the rack!

PRIOR GABRIELLI

I read a text. You wrote it in your book—
"The Cause, the Principle, the One": You speak
Of this Elizabeth of England, who
Usurped the throne, murdered the rightful heir
And blasphemously nominates herself
Head of the Church, Protector of the Faith!

[*he quotes with extra emphasis*]
"I praise her, the Divine Elizabeth,
A queen in title and in dignity,
Whose presence sheds bright light on all the world,
Whom no prince can excel in knowledge, art
Or generosity." The words are yours?

BRUNO

They are.

PRIOR GABRIELLI

The lady is a heretic?

BRUNO

Yes.

PRIOR GABRIELLI

A persecutor of the Church?

BRUNO

Yes!

PRIOR GABRIELLI

And yet to her you dare apply
A title which belongs to God alone:
"Divine"!

[BRUNO *gets a diversion at this moment as the guard brings in the*
cordial and goblet and a tabouret. He sets them up beside BRUNO.
BRUNO *awkwardly tries to pour a drink.*]

MOROSINI
[*to guard*]
Help him, man! For God's sake, help!

[*The guard pours liquor for* BRUNO. *He drinks and hands back the cup. He has had time to collect himself.* MOROSINI *watches him carefully. His reaction is crucial for* MOROSINI.]

BRUNO
[*very carefully*]
My lords, in this I do admit to error.
I should not have praised a heretic.
But consider this in mitigation.
I was much at court—her court!—a guest
Of the Ambassador of France. I hope
You will not make a courtly compliment
A test of orthodoxy!

[*They give him a slight chuckle for this one. He goes on.*]

The epithet
"Divine"? This is the fashion and convention
In a woman's court. A brooch, a ring,
A ribbon or a wig—all are divine!
The Queen herself can hardly merit less!

[*There is another chuckle, but* TAVERNA *stifles it swiftly.*]

TAVERNA
Good Brother Bruno, it would seem you were
More courtier than Christian.

BRUNO
[*humbly*]
Yes, I was,
And I regret it.

TAVERNA
Pause a moment, brother!
You know—none better—in the early Church
The test of faith was to refuse to name
The Emperor "divine."

BRUNO
It was not made
A test in London. Besides, my faith was known
And never abdicated.

TAVERNA
Which was your faith
When you dined out with one Sir Philip Sidney,
To whom you dedicated this—
                    [*he waves the volume.*]
                              —this foul
And monstrous fable, "The Triumphant Beast,"
To satirise the Holy Father?

[BRUNO, *in his weakened state, cannot stand up to the virulence
of the attack. He drifts a moment vaguely, like a stunned fighter.*]

BRUNO
My faith . . . ?
Faith is . . .

[*He slumps in his chair.*]

TAVERNA
Answer, man!

PRIOR GABRIELLI
[*sudden eruption*]
I will not
Endure this tyranny! Nuncio or not,
You are still bound to simple justice. This,
After the rack, is butchery!

TAVERNA
[*sinister and cold*]
Prior,
You forget yourself!

PRIOR GABRIELLI
[*ignores him*]
Eminence!
I call on you, the Shepherd of the Sheep
—The lost ones too! Messer Morosini,
Assessor for the State, you witness this!

MOROSINI
Recorder, set it down! Justice is mocked
If this continues!

PRIOLI
[*the diplomat*]
See to Brother Bruno!

[*The guard and the* RECORDER *go to him; they give him cordial,
bathe his forehead, etc.*]

121

[*to* TAVERNA]
Not long since we reproved a witness here
For lack of charity. I would not see
The Pope, my master, shamed for the same fault
In you.

[TAVERNA *is too canny to fight back. He bows acknowledgement.*]

TAVERNA
I beg an absolution for
My zealotry!

MOROSINI
[*bland*]
We are your colleagues, tell us.
What do you want from Bruno?

TAVERNA
Do we not
All want the same thing? Admission of error,
Rejection of false doctrine, penance and
Reform . . .

PRIOLI
If he offers that, then we,
Good shepherds, take him back into the fold.

MOROSINI
Ask him!

[*All turn to* BRUNO, *who is recovering, and who still manages the graveyard humour.*]

BRUNO

Strange! I felt a sudden slip,
Towards the edge of time. You almost lost me.

TAVERNA
[*calmly*]
Giordano Bruno, are you an honest man?

BRUNO
[*a tired grin*]
By and large I am. Sometimes more by
And sometimes larger. Still, I think at core
I'm honest.

TAVERNA

So we ask you, having a care
For your sick body and your troubled soul,
Will you recant your errors?

[BRUNO *considers the question and summons his strength for a shrewd answer.*]

BRUNO
In general?
Or in particular?

TAVERNA
Why do you ask?

BRUNO

[*summoning his fading strength*]

Because, in general, and truthfully,
I can admit to errors—many of them!
But pin me to particulars—without
A text, or strength for argument, I could
Admit monstrosities. I will not do it.

TAVERNA

Would you, in a penitential time
—And penance would be asked, but clemency
Extended—would you, in sober solitude,
Examine all your texts, confer, reflect
And finally recant what might be shown
False to the Apostolic Doctrine?

[BRUNO *reflects again. He is very tired now.*]

BRUNO

Yes.

I would promise that but not without
The scholar's right of argument.

TAVERNA

Who

Would deny it?

[*to tribunal*]

I am satisfied for now!

[*There is a murmur of agreement round the table.*]

PRIOLI

Approach the table, brother.

[BRUNO *rises with difficulty. He has to be helped by the guard.*]

Kneel!

[*Supporting himself on the table,* BRUNO *kneels painfully.*]

There is
No formulary. Express yourself as if
To God.

[BRUNO *closes his eyes, gathers himself and then staggers through his recantation.*]

BRUNO
My lords, I have, with all sincerity,
Searched heart and conscience and I know that I
Have given cause for scandal and suspicion.
I am ready to reform my life,
Repair the scandal, reject the heresies
I have or may have entertained,
And which I now abhor.
                    [*he begins to break*]
                    For these my sins,
I ask a humble pardon of my God,
Of you, my brethren and superiors,
I willingly accept the punishment
You will determine for me. And I beg . . .
I beg . . . I . . .

[*He breaks and cradles his head on the table, weeping uncontrollably.*]

PRIOLI
[*a ritual question*]
Have you anything else to say?

[*Slowly,* BRUNO *raises his head and looks at him with terrible pathos.*]

BRUNO
No.

There is nothing else!

[PRIOLI *makes a sign to the guard, who leads* BRUNO *like a sleep-walker to his cell. Then* TAVERNA *springs his trap.*]

TAVERNA
A pretty scene!
But Rome will not be satisfied. I serve
A notice on the Church of Venice and the State,
The Holy Office will ask for extradition
Of this notorious heresiarch
For further process of this case!

MOROSINI
[*checkmated and shocked*]
You dare not

Do this!

TAVERNA
I do nothing, sir. I am
A Papal messenger! And you but serve
As State assessor. Let our masters fight

The battle, eh? This is a traders' town,
They'll come to terms! Eminence, good day.

[*He bows and exits, the only victor of the day. The others stare
after him.*]

[*Curtain*]

ACT THREE

Scene I

[*Rome, seven years later.* BRUNO'S *cell in the prison of the Inquisition.*

The cell is furnished with a pallet bed, a table and chair, a stool, in the corner a wooden bucket. On the table there is a single candlestick, quills and ink, a pile of parchment.

It is dawn; a grey light enters from a barred window just at eye-level. The candle is guttering out. BRUNO, *who has worked a great part of the night, is sleeping at the table, head buried on his arms.*

He is seven years older. His hair is greying. He is seamed and scored by his years of confinement. He limps a little as a consequence of his tortures. But throughout this final act, there is a strange, remote calm about him.

There is a rattle of bolts on the cell door. BRUNO *stirs and wakes painfully. The door opens. A* GAOLER *enters with* BRUNO'S *breakfast, a cup of water, bread, a bowl of meal, a spoon. He sets it glumly on the table. Then he crosses to pick up the toilet bucket.*

BRUNO *surveys the breakfast with distaste. He bounces the hard loaf on the table.*]

BRUNO
[*grins*]
When do they bake fresh bread?

GAOLER

Every seven years!

BRUNO

That gives me hope!
I have been here longer than the loaves.
[*he tastes the meal*]
It's cold!

GAOLER

Be glad you're listed with a charity!
Else you'd be eating slops three times a day!

[BRUNO *chuckles. The* GAOLER *goes out, closing the door.*
BRUNO *notices the guttering candle. He blows it out. He makes a
half-hearted effort to eat the meal, dipping the bread into his mug.
Then he pushes it away.*

   *He crumbles some of the bread in his hands, crosses to the
window, stands on the stool and looks out. He whistles a bird-call
and scatters the crumbs on the window ledge. He whistles again.
No birds come.*]

BRUNO

Where are you, little bird? Have you forgotten
Brother Bruno? I wish the others would
Forget him, too. They won't. In Rome, the stones
Remember!
       [*he whistles again, then shivers*]
       When will spring be here? Please,
Fly me a little sun from Africa!
I'm cold.

[*He climbs down stiffly from his stool and returns to the table. He picks up a large official document and scans it wearily.*]

A petition from Giordano Bruno,
Prisoner, unto his Sanctity Pope Clement,
Felicitously reigning . . . Boh! Rejected!

[*He tosses the document down on the table, moves to the bed and flings himself down in utter weariness. He lies staring at the ceiling, talking to himself.*]

Bruno, they have you penned—a silly sheep,
Fly-blown and draggle-tailed. There's no way out
Save through the little gate and down the chute
Into the douche box, where they wash you clean,
Before you join the other happy lambs
In God's green pastures. Is that what you want?
You have it. Just a signature
On Master Bellarmino's document,
A day of public penance in a church,
And you'll be free. . . . Free for what? And who
Then will you be? A cherub with pink cheeks,
A little brainless smile, no body and
A pair of winglets sprouting at the neck?
O God! How they interpret your once grand
Design! . . .

[*Again there is a rattle of bolts, the door opens and the* BARBER *enters. He is a cheery, elderly, talkative fellow, with his bowl and kettle and towel and little bag of instruments. His visit is unexpected.* BRUNO *is delighted to see him. He gets up to greet him.*]

133

Sir Barber! Knight of the shears and razor!

BARBER
[playing a familiar comedy]
Your Eminence! A benediction, please!

BRUNO
God keep your razor sharp, my son, and steady!

BARBER

Amen!

[The BARBER makes a bustle of laying out his tools.]

BRUNO
What brings you here today?

BARBER
[points piously upwards]
                             Orders
From heaven.

BRUNO
Oh-oh! That's ominous!

[The BARBER kicks the cell door shut and then rummages furtively in his bag.]

BARBER
                            I brought
A little something. This!
              [he holds up an orange]

BRUNO
[*delighted*]
Oh no!

BARBER
                    My son
Delivered me a pannier full.

[BRUNO *handles the orange as though it were gold. The* BARBER
is delighted. He fishes again.]

                    And these!

[*He holds up a posy of violets.* Bruno *is hard put to restrain his
tears. He puts down the orange and takes the flowers eagerly.*]

BRUNO
Winter violets . . .

BARBER
                    My little niece
Picked them this morning in the Field of Flowers.

BRUNO
[*caught in a sudden memory*]
"My dear, dear friend, so much a cloudwalker,
You do not see the violets in the grass . . ."

[*The* BARBER *is embarrassed by the emotion.*]

BARBER
They need fresh water!

BRUNO
[*recovers*]
That we have, my friend!

[*He takes his mug, puts the violets in it and sets it on the window ledge.*]

There! They'll share my little light, and I
Will breathe their perfume. Now, Sir Barber, make
Giordano Bruno look like a cardinal!

[*He seats himself, and the* BARBER *goes through all the flourishes of making him ready. He studies him like an artist's model, then begins to clip and talk.*]

BARBER
What shall it be? A tonsure? No, I think
A dash of gallantry . . . We used to have
A fine bright company of cardinals—
Not virtuous, mind, but very colourful,
Plumed hats, slashed hose and crimson velvet cloaks.
. . . Now they're all saints, or if they're not, they're wise
And keep their follies off the streets. It's now
The Jesuits who set the pace! Smart fellows,
Sharp as rapiers, and disciplined . . .

BRUNO
I know. I have their Robert Bellarmino
Writing me love-notes while he cuts me up,
A barber-surgeon for their Holy Office!

BARBER
Why do you fight them? You are getting grey!

You're thin on top! Soon I'll be clipping peach bloom!
Why don't you give them what they want and quit?
Go back to Naples and the sun! There's heart
And music there! We Romans are a stiff
And stubborn bunch—bad haters, too!

BRUNO
[*grins*]
Good Sir Knight, just trim my hair and beard!

BARBER
Mamma! All Southerners have wooden heads!

BRUNO
[*chuckles*]
Now that's a truth!

BARBER
Don't move, I'll chop your ears!
You know the Field of Flowers?

BRUNO
No.

BARBER
That's
Where the violets come from.

BRUNO
Oh!

137

BARBER

Also,
That's where they burn you at the stake, my friend!

BRUNO

Better the violets, eh?

BARBER

You've never seen
A burning?

BRUNO

Nor baited bears, nor killed a bull!

BARBER

Now for the beard. Head back . . . It's quite a day,
To buy a place in front costs gold!

BRUNO

Indeed!

BARBER

Better than Carnival! The whole town's out,
There's a procession, see, from Nona Tower
To the Campo. The fellow for the stake,
He rides an ass. There's guards and pikemen and
A trumpeter. Then there's the Company
Of Mercy—they have a better name, Saint John-
Who-lost-his-head!—they carry relics,
Pictures, crucifixes, so if you want
A final absolution at the stake,
They give it. If you don't, the guards will twist
Your arms and make you seem to kiss the Cross.

If you're obstreperous and make a shout,
They tie your tongue . . . ugh!

BRUNO
                    That's enough!
Just ply the scissors!

BARBER
[*realizing*]
God! I am a fool.

BRUNO
[*gently*]
No! You tell a lively tale! I wonder
How it will read five hundred years from now?
—To make a man confess a loving God
You burn him!

BARBER
          You'll never burn! There's too much sap
In you!

[*He ends his work with a flourish and whips off the towel.*]

          There, now! His Eminence is served!
A mirror!

[BRUNO *surveys himself in the mirror.*]

BRUNO
          Good! I could even meet the Pope,
Provided he would come.

[*The* BARBER *is packing his things.* BRUNO *crosses to him and takes him by the shoulders.*]

        Knight of the Shears,
I cannot pay you. But from my deepest heart,
Thanks for the few hours of liberty
I've known.

[*The* BARBER, *deeply moved, takes his hand and kisses it.*]

       BARBER
     Each time I've come, there has been pain
For you.

       BRUNO
      [*very serious*]
    I tell you something, friend, when I
First came to Rome, I was a nothing man.
In Venice they had me weeping on my knees,
Begging for pity. I've wept here, too—but that's
A different kind of tears. I've begged here, too,
For respite from the torturers. But deep
Inside, a new bud of a man began
To grow—and *you*, my little barber, were
The gardener, you with your clicking scissors,
Clacking tongue, your gifts of laughter and
Your violets, your plums and oranges.
You gave me back my dignity.

       BARBER
       God keep you!

[*He gathers his things awkwardly and hurries out.* BRUNO *stands a moment, deep in thought, then goes to the window, gets down the violets and holds them in his cupped hands, contemplating them.*]

BRUNO

Christ! What a choice to make. To smell the violets
Or the faggot-pile! To walk each day
In the green countryside, to feel the rain
Upon my face, chew on a wheat-stalk,
Watch the tender shoots of next year's grapes
Curl around the vine-poles, and the poplar trees.
—Or else, to make that long, last donkey-ride
Between the pikemen to the stake, to hear
The shouting, and the chant of hypocrites,
To be a spectacle for animals
In human masks!

[*He stiffens in agony, holding the violets as if they are a pillar to support him. The door creaks open and clicks shut, and he turns sharply, to see* PRIOR GABRIELLI *standing against the door. The* PRIOR *has aged too. He is subdued and humble, and yet has increased in dignity.*]

PRIOR GABRIELLI
Brother Bruno.

BRUNO
[*holding himself to formality*]
Prior!

PRIOR GABRIELLI
[*embarrassed*]
Violets! They're blooming in our garden too.

141

BRUNO
[*a touch of irony*]
My barber brought me these.

PRIOR GABRIELLI
May we talk?

BRUNO
[*weary refusal*]
I fear I have spent all my words. I've had
Inquisitors, assessors, counsellors,
Our Master-General, a confessor,
Four advocates and various visitors,
Augustinians and Jesuits,
Friars Discalced and Friars Capuchin,
Persuading me to flee the fire and join
The company of the elect. I crave
A little peace.

PRIOR GABRIELLI
I come, a private man.

[BRUNO *hesitates a moment and then points to the chair.*]

BRUNO
Please, sit down.

[*The* PRIOR *seats himself behind the table.* BRUNO *perches on the corner of it, begins to juggle the orange and then to peel it.*]

PRIOR GABRIELLI
I was the man who gave
To Mocenigo the notion of betrayal.

BRUNO
[*ignores the admission*]
How is my lady?

PRIOR GABRIELLI
Well, and yet, not well.
There is no loving in that house, and you—
The memory of what was done to you—
Haunts every hallway.

BRUNO
Tell her from me—tell her—
What little calm I have, she gave. What grace
I find in this so graceless world is hers.

PRIOR GABRIELLI
I promise that.

BRUNO
Taverna, Morosini,
Mocenigo?

PRIOR GABRIELLI
These are straw men, blown
By every wind of power.

BRUNO
I clutch at straws,
A man in a wild river crying "Help"
—And no one hears!

PRIOR GABRIELLI
[*hesitant*]
Bruno!

BRUNO
Yes?

PRIOR GABRIELLI
To say I pity you would be a slight
Upon us both. Never in all my life
Have I known such a man. I hate what you
Profess. You I admire as being more—
Much more—a man, and more believer, too,
Than half the canting orthodox. But, Bruno,
You are such a numbskull! A billy-goat
Butting his head against the bastions
Of Castel Angelo. That's the Pope's
Own fortress. Who must win, the billy-goat
Or the Pope?

[BRUNO *grins and pops a slice of orange into his mouth.*]

BRUNO
A billy-goat! Now there's a name
for Bruno!

PRIOR GABRIELLI
And have you ever found a name
For me?

BRUNO
[*a moment's reflection*]
Yes. I think I have. You are
A man who has a talent for belief.
You're fortunate. Give you good premises,
You'll draw a safe conclusion. Then you pull
The shutters down and say: "The light is plenty

For the road to Paradise." Hand you
A torch, you'll set the world on fire and call it
Christendom, no matter who gets burned.

PRIOR GABRIELLI

Not bad! And yet I envy you, and you,
I think, do sometimes envy me!

[BRUNO *hands him a piece of orange. He accepts it.*]

BRUNO
I do.
That's a good orange. My first since God knows when!

PRIOR GABRIELLI
[*munching*]
I disapprove of all this cruelty.

BRUNO
[*attacks*]
And yet—so the Pope puts his name to it,
Or with a God-like gesture shrugs it off
Onto the civil state—you will accept
The last brutality?

PRIOR GABRIELLI
If I do not,
Who tells me then, good Bruno, right and wrong?

BRUNO

Is it necessary?

PRIOR GABRIELLI
Yes! How else
Can we comport ourselves as Christian men?

BRUNO
Look at the document before you.

[*The* PRIOR *picks up the parchment and scans it.*]

PRIOR GABRIELLI
I saw it
At the Holy Office.

BRUNO
Those are eight
Separate propositions from my books
Declared heretical.

PRIOR GABRIELLI
In fact, they are.

BRUNO
Who says so?

PRIOR GABRIELLI
Bellarmino and the best
Of all our theologians.

BRUNO
Honest men,
I have no doubt of it. But tell me, Prior,
Who says God whispers in their ears? Who says
That Bellarmino is infallible?

PRIOR GABRIELLI
The Pope accepts his verdict.

BRUNO
                    But the Pope
Has never read a single line of all
My treatises. How can he judge the frame
In which I speak? Even the language!
I'm a Nolan. I could dazzle you
In dialect, because the words do not
Make the same sense to different men. Our Popes
—Now tell me honestly—have they
The gift of tongues?

PRIOR GABRIELLI
[*wry*]
God help us! No!

BRUNO
Now here's the terror of it! Here are you
And here am I, munching a juicy orange.
Am I a devil with a pitchfork tail?

PRIOR GABRIELLI
No!

BRUNO
    Could you believe that I might be
In purest conscience before God—if not
The Church?

PRIOR GABRIELLI
        I could.

BRUNO
            And could you, as they propose,
For that clear conscience—kill me?

PRIOR GABRIELLI
                  Never! No!

BRUNO
Suppose I kneel now and say to you,
Good Prior, there may be doubts, but I have none,
Give me the sacrament, absolve me from
My sins. What will you do, as confessor?

PRIOR GABRIELLI
I will absolve you in the same good faith.

BRUNO
And I'll accept the absolution—if
You'll walk tomorrow to the stake with me!

[*The* PRIOR *is deeply shocked.*]

PRIOR GABRIELLI
To make what affirmation?

BRUNO
                  Only this!
To shout abroad that God Almighty made
Of every man a self. This was the first
Gift and the last. And we, to hold that gift
Safe for our brothers and our sons—must die!

[*There is a long pause. The* PRIOR *holds up the document.*]

PRIOR GABRIELLI

What have you done with this?

BRUNO

Nothing—yet!

PRIOR GABRIELLI

Then sign while there is time. They want you free!
You are a shame to them. Accept the key.
Walk out into the daylight and forget
The sad and sterile years of argument.

BRUNO
[*very quiet*]

I, too, want to be free. I have not seen
The sun for seven years. I have—by Christ—
Made test of every compromise by which
I still might sign and keep a single shred
Of self-hood. —And they come this very day
To ask my answer.

PRIOR GABRIELLI

Give them "No," my friend,
And you are dead!

BRUNO

It is not death I fear.
Already I have died a dozen deaths,
Waiting for torture and the questioning.
The terror that haunts me is quite different:

To see and know, on that last Calvary,
The ultimate malice of inventive man!
                    [*a terrible summation*]
They will make me a clown before I die.

[*The* PRIOR *agrees. He gropes for a word of consolation. He finds
a paradox.*]

                    PRIOR GABRIELLI
Christ died a clown! —A cardboard king, his crown
A twist of briar thorns.

                    BRUNO
                    [*muses on it*]
                    Perhaps he was.
Perhaps that is the truth of it, that man
And only man can mock himself—and mock
The artifacts he calls divinities.

[*There is a pause.*]

                    PRIOR GABRIELLI
If you wish, I'll bear you company
Until they come.

                    BRUNO
                    [*touched*]
                    Prior, my thanks, but truly,
I am a braver man alone, without
An audience for my loose and braggart tongue.

[*The* PRIOR *gets up heavily, crosses to* BRUNO. *Then he fishes in his habit and brings out his breviary. He hands it to* BRUNO. BRUNO *accepts it.*]

PRIOR GABRIELLI
If you would like to pray, this is my book.

BRUNO
[*moved and savage*]
I do not wish to pray. Be there a God,
He has a debt to me and, being just,
Will pay it. If there be no God,
          [*a real agony*]
No prayer, no incantation will assuage
The monstrous agony of human kind.
          [*relaxes*]
But I will keep the book for brotherhood.

[*There is a sound of measured footfalls. They both turn. Three Curial Officials and two armed guards enter the cell. One of the officials is a* NOTARY. *He carries a rolled document.*]

NOTARY
Giordano Bruno?

BRUNO
     Myself.

NOTARY
          I am required
To put a question.

BRUNO
[*controlled*]
I know the question, sir.
I need a moment's quiet.

[*The* NOTARY *bows assent.* BRUNO *turns away and moves to the window. He bows his head, puts hands to forehead to still the beating inside his skull. After a long moment he turns, haggard but challenging.*]

Let us be clear!
This is what you ask: "Rejoin the flock,
Recite the Creeds. Deny what once you wrote,
Believing it was true. Then make an act
Of public penitence—we'll let you live!
Refuse, we kill you!" That's the nub of it!

[*No one challenges his interpretation. After a long pause, he goes on quietly.*]

Which of you gentlemen begot me? Which
Breathed into this sack of bones the life
I did not ask for? None of you? Who then?
Aldobrandini, who is now the Pope?
Did Bellarmino? Any cardinal
Of the Inquisitors? Who said to me,
A foetus in the womb, a puling babe,
"You have your life, but on the condition that
You thus believe?" No one! Not even God!
So, gentlemen, I say you have no right
To make terms for my life. I tell you then—
No! I will not recant. I will not sign!

[*The* NOTARY *simply nods, unrolls his parchment and begins to* *read. The sentence which he reads is the actual one passed upon* GIORDANO BRUNO, *and the formal prose must be delivered in* *such a fashion as to match, but be different from, the blank verse* *of the rest of the play. It must convey by its very legalism the* *enormity of* BRUNO'*s fate.*]

NOTARY

Having invoked the name of our Lord Jesus Christ
And of his most Glorious Mother Mary ever Virgin
In the cause of the aforesaid causes
Brought before this Holy Office
Between, on the one hand,
The Procurator Fiscal of the said Holy Office,
And on the other hand, yourself,
The aforesaid Giordano Bruno the accused,
Examined, brought to trial
And found guilty, impenitent,
Obstinate and pertinacious,
In this, our sentence,
Determined by the counsel and opinion of our advisers,
The Reverend Fathers,
Masters in Sacred Theology and Doctors in both laws,
We hereby, in these documents,
Publish, announce, pronounce, sentence,
And declare you Brother Giordano Bruno,
To be an impenitent heretic,
And therefore to have incurred
All the ecclesiastical censures
And pains of the Holy Canon,
The laws and the constitutions,
Both general and particular,
Imposed on such

Confessed impenitent, pertinacious
And obstinate heretics,
Wherefore as such we verbally degrade you
And declare that you must be degraded,
And we hereby ordain and command
That you shall be actually degraded
From all your ecclesiastical orders
Both major and minor
In which you have been ordained,
According to the Sacred Canon Law;
And that you must be driven forth,
And we do drive you forth
From our ecclesiastical forum
And from our Holy and Immaculate Church
Of whose mercy you have become unworthy.
And we ordain and command
That you must be delivered to the Secular Court
         [*he pronounces the terrible and hypocritical irony*]
That you may be punished
With the punishment deserved,
Though we earnestly pray

That it will mitigate the
Rigour of the laws
Concerning the pains of your person,
That you may not be in danger of death
Or of mutilation of your members.
Furthermore, we condemn,
We reprobate and we prohibit
All your aforesaid and your other books and writings
As heretical and erroneous,
Containing many heresies and errors,
And we ordain that all of them

Which have come or may in future come
Into the hands of the Holy Office
Shall be publicly destroyed and burned
Upon the Square of St. Peter,
Before the steps,
And that they shall be placed
On the Index of Forbidden Books.
And as we have commanded, so shall it be done.
And thus we say, pronounce, sentence, declare,
Degrade, command and ordain,
We chase forth and deliver
And we pray in this
And in every other better method and form
That we reasonably can and should.
Thus pronounce we
The Cardinal General Inquisitors,
Whose names subscribe this document.

[*The* NOTARY *rolls up his parchment.*]

From this moment, you are, as to your body,
At the disposal of the Secular Court.
As to your soul, may God have mercy on you.

[BRUNO *digests the terrible words and then nods slowly.*]

BRUNO
At this moment, gentlemen, I think
That you are more afraid of me than I
Of you.

[*Then, with the old monastic gesture of retirement, he pulls his* cowl up over his face and stands, holding the book, in the attitude of the statue in the Campo dei Fiori.

The others withdraw and leave him alone.

The lights change. As they do, he seems to turn into stone, a defiant figure, permanently accusing tyranny.]

[The Curtain Falls]

MORRIS L. WEST, a native Australian, was born in Melbourne in 1916. When he was fourteen he began studying as a postulant with the Christian Brothers order but left twelve years later without having taken final vows. After serving with Australian Army Intelligence during World War II, he became a partner in a flourishing recording and transcription business but left it when he discovered that he preferred to write for himself rather than for sponsors.

A stay in Italy resulted in his book *Children of the Sun*, a study of the street urchins of Naples, which became an English best seller in 1957. There followed two novels published in the United States under the titles *The Crooked Road* and *Backlash*, in 1957 and 1958 respectively.

In 1958, also, Mr. West returned to Italy as Vatican correspondent for *The Daily Mail*, and he then absorbed much of the technical background for a new novel. *The Devil's Advocate*, published in 1959, promptly became that rare phenomenon in publishing—a book universally hailed by critics as a major creative work while selling, in various editions, more than two million copies. Mr. West followed it with more major successes: *Daughter of Silence* (1962), *The Shoes of the Fisherman* (1963), *The Ambassador* (1965), and *The Tower of Babel* (1968).

Mr. West, with his wife and four children, presently lives in Rome, Italy.

Acknowledgements

The research for this play was prepared and collated by my son, Julian West, and is based upon the following works:

McIntyre, J. L., *Giordano Bruno* (Macmillan, 1903)

Singer, D. W., *Giordano Bruno; His Life and Thoughts* (Schumann, 1950)

Yates, F. A., *Giordano Bruno and the Hermetic Tradition* (Routledge, 1964)

Spampanato, V. (ed.), *Documenti Della Vita di Giordano Bruno* (Florence, 1933)

Firpo, L., *Il Processo di Giordano Bruno* (Naples, 1933)

Mercati, A. (ed.), *Il Sommario del Processo di Giordano Bruno* (Città del Vaticano, 1942)

Horowitz, I. L., *The Renaissance Philosophy of Giordano Bruno* (Coleman-Ross, 1952)

Nelson, J. C., *Renaissance Theory of Love* (Columbia University Press, 1958)

Giordano Bruno, *The Expulsion of the Triumphant Beast*. Transl. by Imerti, A. D. (Rutgers University Press, 1964)

Giordano Bruno, *Cause, Principle and Unity*. Transl. by Lindsay, J. (International Pubs., 1962)

Giordano Bruno, *On the Infinite Universe and Worlds*. Transl. by Singer, D. W. (in Singer's *Giordano Bruno: His Life and Thoughts*)

Articles in the following encyclopaedias:
Britannica, Colliers, Catholic.

The responsibility for the characterisations and inventions in this play is that of the Author.

Set in Fotosetter Biretta
by Westcott & Thomson, Inc.
Printed on Sulgrave Laid paper by
Rae Publishing Company and
bound by The Haddon Craftsmen, Inc.
Designed by Lucy Mahoney